Agnes White

Gordon Lodge or Retribution

An Autobiography

Agnes White

Gordon Lodge or Retribution
An Autobiography

ISBN/EAN: 9783741133763

Manufactured in Europe, USA, Canada, Australia, Japa

Cover: Foto ©Andreas Hilbeck / pixelio.de

Manufactured and distributed by brebook publishing software (www.brebook.com)

Agnes White

Gordon Lodge or Retribution

GORDON LODGE

OR,

RETRIBUTION.

AN AUTOBIOGRAPHY.

BY

MISS M. AGNES WHITE,

Of West Virginia.

BALTIMORE:
KELLY, PIET AND COMPANY,
174 W. Baltimore Street.
1873.

PREFACE.

Some writer has said that the preface is the best part of a book. Now I should dislike very much to think that it formed the best part of this volume that I have given to the public with so many misgivings. My excuses in writing this little story are simple these: To while away the lonely wintry hours in the mountain, and to entertain in a measure the fireside group. I had no idea at the time it would go to the press, but at the urgent request of a friend was prevailed upon to send it, and found to my satisfaction that it was kindly received.

If my readers will find any pleasure in its perusal, I shall be much pleased, and will be amply rewarded for the labor it cost me.

DEDICATION.

WITH PROUD LOVE AND REVERENCE

FOR

HER TENDER CARE,

I WITH SINCERE AFFECTION

DEDICATE

THIS LITTLE VOLUME

TO

MY DEAR MOTHER.

GORDON LODGE;

OR,

RETRIBUTION.

CHAPTER I.

JOHN INTRODUCES HIMSELF AND PARENTS TO HIS READERS.

Y name is *John*, and a very romantic name it is, and the most romantic old fellow in the world, I think, possesses it; besides, I am not handsome, attractive, captivating, comely, endearing, graceful, charming, or magnificent John. No, indeed, far from it; on the contrary, I am and have been called homely, awkward, unprepossessing, and ungraceful John. Now this is right hard to bear, don't you think? Who is it that does not love to be praised and admired? and who is it that likes to be called repulsive and ugly? In all this wide world I do not think there is one; and everyone becomes indignant that is so called, whether they

deserve it or not. Oh! how angry I must have been sometimes when I was a little boy; but then there were times, too, when I would hear some very soothing remarks about my poor self, which would make me feel much grander in my own estimation, such as, "John Meredith is one of the noblest works of God; he is an honest boy and will be an honest man." I would not feel quite so much like the "ugly, little duck" when these pleasing speeches would reach my ears; I would walk bold and erect, and felt capable of looking the Lord Lieutenant straight in the face, which the fear of my ugly phiz (astonishing people often) prevents me doing. But compliments make us bold, there is no two ways about it, and even I, after hearing them, could hold up my head and walk with as much confidence as if I were the best-looking man alive, and look people straight in the face with my great, green eyes, which my poor dead mother thought much more beautiful and expressive than those of any blooming country lass or charming city belle. But I was never handsome or attractive. I am sensible enough to know that. So pray, good readers, do not be troubled or uneasy, and imagine that I am going to introduce to you a *Hero*, whose name was John (poor, unpretending name), who was unfortunate enough to have an awkward figure, great hands, great feet, and the feature which is most prominent in everybody's face being unusually so in mine. It is a fact, dear reader, that a big nose is a sad thing, being only better than no nose at all. So I always thought. But I am a very happy old man now, and quite used to the name of John; particularly so, since a pair of dimpled arms entwined themselves lovingly around my old neck, not many days ago, giving me a great hug, and the owner saying: "I love the name of John; it is so easy to call, and all dear old people ought to be called John, too." Now don't come to the hasty conclusion, my friends, that these little arms belong to me. Oh! no such thing; but you shall hear all about them as I go along and tell "the old man's story."

I must go back far into the past, over many, many eventful years, with their black, lowering clouds and heavy storms that bowed the great oak and crushed the slender lily. It is sad to think over events which were fraught with sorrow, but the little Fairy, who said she loved even my name, and who lingers round the "old man," ministering to him, smoothing his hoary locks and kissing his wrinkled forehead, requests it, and I am a doating old man enough to sit down and spend a couple of hours every day for my little darling's entertainment. First, then, in commencing, I must, in justice to myself, tell you who I am, what I am and where I came from.

I was born in merry, old England, in a pretty white cottage situated in a very verdant, fertile valley, not many miles from the celebrated Thames. It was there that I saw the first peep of daylight, uttered the first sound that escaped from my lips, took my first steps, got the first thump on my big head, learned to hum that very charming old English nursery song, "Pollie, put the kettle on," and then in the little green yard, spangled with its buttercups and daisies (as I last remember it), I flew my kites, rode my stick horses to water, romped with my dog, played "hide and seek" with my goat, and would lie down on the soft, velvet grass, with violets for a pillow, and sleep, with my pet lambs, the sleep of innocence. Nor were my morning and evening prayers forgotten; for at my mother's knee I repeated them, looking up into her lovely face, which mirrowed her beautiful soul, and learned, or tried to learn, to love and please God. Ah! if every mother knew how her gentle voice and gentle warnings sank into her son's heart, and how, in after years, those gentle warnings were listened to, she would double them, and never lose an opportunity to teach him to know and love God. My dear mother thought her son John a very promising lad, and treasured me and loved me. I used to compare myself to a huge cabbage rose, in the possession of an old woman who lived near us, and who prized this great, unlovely flower as the city gardener loves and tends his hot-house, with its virgin white camelias, tender Nile lilies, blushing roses, fragrant hyacinths and delicate fringed fuchsias. But I, like the cabbage rose, needed little attention. I was sturdy and strong, braving the winter winds, the hoary frosts and driving rain without the least inconvenience from colds or chills. Being the only child, of course I was a darling; and I don't think my devoted parents knew that I was ugly. But I must give a short sketch of my father and mother's life before I proceed with my own.

My mother was the second daughter of an English gentleman, who had been left a widower whilst still a young man, having the responsibility of two pretty little daughters, to whom he devoted his life. In course of time the little girls, as all little girls do, grew up to be young ladies and got married. The eldest, Mary, married a United States Navy Captain, and went to the great Republic to live; here I drop all further mention of this aunt of mine, as I heard very little of her after my mother's death, but think she died shortly after her arrival in America. My mother was some years younger than her sister, was very lovely, quite an heiress and well connected. My father was the son of an English barrister, Mr. James Meredith. He was an unusually fine-looking young man, as the portrait which hangs not far from here has told me, very prepossessing in appearance (which legacy he forgot to bequeath to his poor son), and an oratorical genius; at an early age he was admitted to the bar and was completely lionized. Country cousins swarmed around him as bees around the sweetest flower. Sisters were completely lost in admiration at this model of a young man, with his many graces and winning address. How it was that I was so ugly goodness only knows, when both my mother and father were so peerless, except as grammarians explain it, on the principle that "two negatives are equivalent to an affirmative;" but I am comforted by the old adage, "Pretty is as pretty does." My father was a poor young man up to the time he married my mother; so in marrying her, he won both a fortune and a beauty. The meeting took place as follows:

It was on a lovely May evening in 17—, when the rising moon, throwing its brilliant beams on the rivers, kissed them into silver as they went eddying and hurrying to the sea, that a gentleman drew up at an inn in the rising town of B——. The handsome vehicle, drawn by full-blooded, restive, black horses, were stared at and admired by crowds of little urchins, who were all honestly wishing "they were rich and could ride." As the gentleman alighted, he handed out a maiden who, throwing back her veil, revealed "as fair a face as ere was seen." The arrival created quite a sensation, for a gentleman with a bearing so noble, and a lady so beautiful, had not been seen in B—— for many a long day. So as hastily as domestics could arrange and put in order, the best rooms in the hotel were prepared and made comfortable for the reception of the distinguished guests who had made such an impression on the community.

"Well, landlord," said the new arrival, as he found himself seated upon the open piazza opposite the worthy host, after paying the necessary attention to his young traveling companion, "you seem to be right quiet here in your little town; not much, I suppose, to break the monotony?"

"Well, no," answered the landlord, taking his pipe from his mouth and blowing a great puff of smoke upwards; "there is not a great deal, to be sure; but now and then there is a little excitement, and to-night, I believe, there is to be a slight variation."

"In what way?" asked the guest; "an opera company, or anything of that kind?" thinking at the time of the young lady.

"No, no," said the host, "not quite so grand as that;

but a fine speech from a talented young barrister, who seems to be making quite a name for himself. His subjects are well chosen and his address most favorable."

"Ah! I should like very much to hear him, and think my little daughter would not object to it either; I shall go and see."

"It can't be possible," said the facetious landlord, "that the young lady is the daughter of so young a gentleman as yourself? Why, I would not suppose such a thing."

"Oh, yes!" said the guest, with a pleased smile, thinking the host very agreeable; "oh, yes! she is my own daughter, and has a sister some years older than herself."

"Well, well," said the landlord, "I should never believe it if I had not heard it from your own lips."

The gentleman bowed, in acknowledgement to the compliment, and withdrew to his daughter's room.

"You may come in," said a soft voice, in answer to his knock; "I am not asleep."

"I am glad of it," said he, entering. "Are you fatigued, my little dear?"

"No, indeed. I feel as fresh as the morn," laughing, and catching his hands affectionately; "and how does my papa feel?"

"Not quite so fresh as my pretty daughter; though, of course, it wouldn't be supposed that an old man should feel like a young lady of eighteen; but, nevertheless, I am first-rate."

"You shan't call yourself old," said the young lady, playfully putting her hands over his mouth; "you are not old, you are just as young-looking and handsome as anybody."

"Oh! yes, little flatterer; that sounds mighty sweet from your pretty lips, but the old glass, there, is not such a story-teller. I have come to take you to the Hall, where there is to be a fine speech delivered by a rising star, a second Demosthenes, and to be given, I believe, for some charitable purpose. Are you willing to go? Would you like it? We shall be here for several days, so you shall know this famous orator and coquet with him as much as you please, so that you won't be lonesome while my business detains me."

"For shame, papa! I would not coquet with anybody. You surely would not accuse me of such a thing! Why, what do you suppose I am made of?"

"Why, what all other young ladies are made of, pretty one. What else should you be made of?"

"You are a naughty, teasing papa to say your daughter is a flirt. For shame! Never mind; I will not give you a chance to say such things of me much longer. I'm going to marry the first one that will ask me, even if it is this great orator, just to prove to you that you are maligning your daughter in a most fearful manner."

The father laughed, and patting her on the head, said, playfully: "Well, well, come on, now, and I won't tease any more if you will only hurry and put on your bonnet, for it is nearly time."

"I'll be ready in a few minutes. Just let me put this flower in my hair, for you know this Demosthenes must fall in love with me, and little flowers are great attractions."

"Especially when they are such flowers as I possess," returned the fond father, taking her hand and placing it in his arm.

"That compliment is just as sweet as my darling papa," she said, as they passed out together.

The hall in which the young barrister, James Meredith, was to speak was large, brilliantly illuminated, and decorated with the first spring flowers, wreathed with sprays of arbor vitæ, which hung in graceful garlands all around the spacious apartment. It was well filled with the youth and beauty of the town, arrayed in their finest apparel. The English gentleman and his daughter were honored with pleasant seats, and in which the young lady's charms were shown to the best advantage. Nor was my grandfather ashamed of the fair young creature that was seated beside him, oh! no; on the contrary, he was both pleased and proud, as on every side he met glances of admiration cast upon her: and if my mother (for you must know by this time that the pretty girl was no other than she, for I would not be tasking myself to tell you of people who lived and loved before I was born unless I was deeply interested in them, and who could I be more interested in than in my parents?) showed to advantage, my father did too; for I have been told that never in the town of B——, or out of it, was such an oration listened to with such attention and marked approval. And as the bouquets of beautiful flowers fell upon the stage, my mother snatched the tiny blossom from her own sunny hair and threw it at his feet, where he singled it out from the rest, smiling with pleasure, bowed low and gracefully in acknowledgement, and placed it in his bosom.

I am not going to linger long over my parents' courtship, for, since the days of Adam, the sameness in courtships makes all, except your own particular one, tiresome. Suffice it to say that, in their case, the course of true love ran smoothly enough; for my grandfather liked and admired the young genius, and was far too indulgent to his favorite child to deny her one single wish. So, eighteen months from the night of which I have just spoken, they were married. My grandfather lived but a short time after the happy pair were wed, and my mother left his city home in London and came to the little cottage where I was born, and which, after many years of absence, is still so dear to me from the memories of the past. There, up to the age of thirteen, I spent my happiest days. My parents were devoted to their only child, and spared me every possible pain, and often in my troubles through life have I looked back on those bright, bright years with a weary longing for their return.

At thirteen my sorrows began—an early age, truly, for a heart to learn woe—and those whom I most dearly prized in life had shadows cast on their young lives; but I will not anticipate.

CHAPTER II.

JOHN LOSES HIS PARENTS.

THE sered and yellow leaves of autumn were beginning to fall, covering the little yard like a variegated carpet, rustling softly with each passing breeze. On the evening of a day in the year 18—, which stands out very plainly to my memory, my mother drew her chair to the cheerful fire, and cast an anxious glance at the soft grey of the sky, wondering why her husband did not return. He had been absent for some days, called away on urgent business. Her face was sad and very thoughtful, but, oh! so tender and loving that the anxiety depicted on it made me love her more, and running to her, I asked: "What troubles you, dear mother?" and as I spoke I saw the tears coming into her soft blue eyes.

"My little son," she answered, tenderly, laying my head on her bosom, "there is a great weight here (placing her hand on her heart), a weight that is crushing me, and I have a presentiment of coming evil."

"But, mother," I said, rising and sitting on her knee, "I am sure we are very happy, so why should you be sad? Haven't we had everything we wanted? and hasn't God been mighty good to us?"

"Yes, yes, darling, He truly has," she replied; "but we must not expect to be happy always; as our Redeemer bore His cross, so we must carry ours; and we should never forget that we are the followers of a crucified Saviour. But, ah! my son, even these reflections cannot remove this feeling of uneasiness, and it makes me very unhappy."

"Dearest," she continued, after a few moments' pause, "if anything were to happen to rob you of your father and mother, what would become of you, my child, all alone in this wretched world? Oh! my darling, the thought of this is what makes your mother so miserable."

"Then, mother, it is because you love *me* that you are unhappy! Do you really love me so very much, dear mother?"

"Love you, dearest? There is not a hair of this dear head that I do not fondly love," brushing at the same time with her gentle touch the unruly curls back from my forehead.

It seems as if it ran in our family to be forewarned of coming events. I have often been since then, and can fully sympathize with and understand now how my poor mother felt on that October evening so long ago; for she felt that, should anything happen her or my father, in this cold world there were few or any that would care for her lonely boy.

I had just laid my cheek against her soft face, pressing her fair hand to my lips, and asked her to smile again and comfort her child's heart (for I was truly unhappy at seeing her so sorrowful), and she had only time to answer my request by smiling on me so sweetly that it brightened up all those lovely features (alas! my mother's last smile), when the door opened, and my father, pale, trembling, and exhausted, entered and threw himself into the nearest chair. My mother flew to his side, in agony exclaiming: "My husband! my husband! what is it?" His head dropped wearily on his shoulder as he answered with a groan of pain. Frightened and troubled, I hastened to him and caught his hand in my own. Never had I felt such a burning palm. It horrified me. Never shall I forget it, or the picture my parents presented. My father, with his noble brow contracted with deep pain, leaning his throbbing head on my mother's slender shoulder, whilst she, with eyes wild with despair and arms clasped convulsively around him, wept as only a loving wife can weep at seeing death written upon the face of her husband. I stood mute and motionless, not knowing, and yet don't know, which I felt for most, my father passing away whilst yet in the prime of life, or my poor sorrow-stricken mother. After a few moments my father spoke:

"Dear wife," said he, "do not grieve; cease weeping and sorrowing; try to be resigned to our Heavenly Father's will; for the decree has gone forth, and I must die; this disease will not spare me longer; try to be calm for my sake."

"Hush, oh! hush; do not say that you are going to leave me," sobbed my mother. "You will not, shall not leave me. Do not say those awful words again or they will kill me. Oh, my merciful Saviour, do not take my husband from me!"

She stopped suddenly in her wild cry, for she saw that her terror and excitement were increasing the fearful fever which my father had; this subdued her at once, and, weeping silently, she leaned her face on her husband's bowed head. I thought my father was sleeping, he remained quiet so long. I feared to move, but at last he called my name feebly.

"Son," he spoke, "I am soon to leave you. It is a bitter trial to part from you, my dear boy, but the will of God must be accomplished. Learn, then, to pray that that mighty will will always be accomplished in you. This is all I ask of you, my child, and all you need to be a perfect Christian. Do you promise me, John?"

"Yes, father," I answered, weeping. He held his hand towards me; I caught it to my lips; a smile, as a faint sunbeam, lit his face as he heard my answer; then all was quiet.

The next evening, ere the sun had gone to rest, they had laid him quietly away in the lonely churchyard to "sleep the sleep that knows no wakening."

I felt that I could bear this sorrow, for my mother was left; but as days, weeks, and months passed away without bringing one smile to her lips, and her cheek grew pale and thinner, I became alarmed, for after one grief has come to us, we instinctively fear and dread another; and every day I trembled with fear lest she would be taken from me too. And, oh! how those forebodings were realized! for one soft May evening, only ten months after my father's death, the parting came. I did not know she had been so sick, so gently and silently she faded away just as the early flowers came into bloom. She called me to her bedside, saying, softly:

"Darling, don't leave me any more. I will not be with you long."

"What do you mean, mother?" I asked, looking into her tender eyes whilst one of my old fears came upon me.

"I mean, my child, that I am going to leave you."

"Then take me with you," I cried, in childish innocence.

"Would to God I could, my pet lamb. Oh, then, how happily I would go. All that grieves me is leaving you."

"Then, where are you going, mother dear?" I asked, leaning against the bed.

"To see your father in heaven, darling," she said, whilst tears chased each other down her pale, delicate face.

For the first time the whole dreadful truth flashed upon me, my head began to swim, and I would have fallen but her sweet voice recalled me, and with an effort I controlled myself.

"My dearest one," she said, slowly, "I recommend you to the care and protection of your Redeemer. After I am no more, you will be taken to your cousin, Sir Clarence Graham, and with him you will live until you are of age; then you will come into possession of your property, which is very valuable. Now, don't sob so, my poor, poor boy, but pray our sweet Saviour to comfort you, and give me your hand and promise me to live in peace with both God and man."

Weeping, I obeyed. She then drew my head to her and pressed a long, lingering kiss upon my forehead; then clasping her hands upon her breast, her lovely spirit took its flight as the sweet name of Jesus passed her lips

CHAPTER III.

JOHN MAKES THE ACQUAINTANCE OF HIS COUSINS.

DON'T be tired of me, dear friends, for I must introduce myself to you right often before my story finishes.

My life, though dark and stormy, has had its gleams of sunshine here and there to brighten it, as sometimes we can catch a glimpse of heaven's blue when the sky is o'ercast with the heaviest, blackest clouds, and the bright flashes of electricity illuminating the scene makes us oblivious for the moment of the gloominess of the path it travels.

It was only darkness to me everywhere when my mother was laid to sleep, and as I threw myself upon the new-made grave with a cry of agony and pain, I thought my heart was breaking. And why didn't it? I have asked myself since. If it only had, what a life of sorrow would have been spared me. With my face buried in my hands and my heart in my mother's coffin, I leaned upon the cold clay, with the evening sunbeams playing through the trees, making cheerful all things except my young life. "Mother, will you never come back?" I asked again and again, and each time the distant hills echoed *never*. Gradually, in addition to the pain of being forever separated from her, a sense of loneliness and want came over me, and I began to realize that I was indeed alone, with no kind friend to help me, when a hand was gently placed on my shoulder, and a low voice said:

"Don't be so sad, my child. You shall come with me and I will take care of you."

I rose from my kneeling posture, and confronted a richly dressed and handsome gentleman. I was too young then and too deeply grieved to think of much, but his elegant dress struck my fancy instantly, and for a moment I forgot that I stood by my mother's last resting place, so completely lost in wonder at the beautiful dress, with its great, shining buttons, brilliant studs, massive chain, and beautiful shirt frills. I thought I had never seen anything so magnificent before, and almost fancied myself in the presence of some prince from fairy land. The enchantment was broken by the gentleman taking my hand and saying:

"My poor little boy, you have suffered a great loss; but come with me and I will take you to my pretty home and try to make you happy. I am your cousin, Sir Clarence Graham, your mother's only living relative and now your protector. Come quietly away; this is not a good place for you; it will make you think too much of your poor mother."

The latter part of this speech I thought very unkind. Why should I not think of my mother? Though I was much embarrassed at being in the presence of so great a person as Sir Clarence, still I was not too much so to say: "I will think of my mother as much as I want to. Wasn't she my mother and didn't she love me more than any one else?" Here I completely broke down and sobbed so violently that my cousin became alarmed.

"Don't cry," he said, soothingly; "it will make you

sick, and you won't be able to take the long journey that is before you. Come now," and taking my hand in his, lead me back to my home.

It did not take Sir Clarence long to make arrangements for our departure, for he seemed anxious to be gone, whilst I was thinking of the two graves in the quiet churchyard and clinging to each old servant as they gathered around to bid the little orphan good-bye, as if their kind hands could keep me forever near the place where my mother and father rested.

"This won't do, my boy," said Sir Clarence, rather hastily, as he saw me sobbing on the neck of my old nurse, whilst she, in broken accents, was lamenting my departure. "This won't do, *this won't do*," he kept repeating as he took me by the hand and led me away. "Come, child, come, we do not want to be all night traveling. You must come sometime and just as well now as any other."

And so I went away, parted from my native land and that little home that had been my shelter from infancy, where the wild rose and honey-suckle, climbing over the lattice, formed such a sweet and rustic picture, whilst all around spoke of peace and quiet, loveliness and repose.

I leaned from the carriage window as I heard my old Scotch terrier whine after me, and as I did so, the big white cat sprang upon the gate post with a mew, intended, I thought, for a farewell; even the chickens, ducks and geese flew after the vehicle, as if to bid adieu to their little master, and as my eyes caught a last glimpse of the great trees that surrounded my home, and of the river Thames, on whose bosom several white sails were visible, I laid my head down in the corner of the carriage and wept myself to sleep.

I know not how long I slept, but when I opened my eyes I found my cousin reading the newspaper very quietly, and apparently oblivious of my existence.

I was both heart-sore and weary as the evening advanced, and had begun to wonder how I could live with Sir Clarence if he never spoke to me, when he suddenly raised his head and somewhat startled me by asking:

"Are you tired, child?"

"Yes," I answered, "very tired."

"I am sorry," was the brief reply, as he continued his reading. What a queer man, I thought. I would like to know what he finds so interesting in that paper. Maybe he can't speak much English. Mamma told me he lived in Ireland. I continued thinking a great deal, looking all the time at my cousin, till at length he laid down his paper and asked:

"Well, John, how do you think you will like living in old Ireland?"

"I don't know," I answered; "will I have to live there long?"

"Yes, I suppose so," he returned; "but I think you will like it when you see my little girls and get acquainted with them."

"Little girls!" I said. "Where are they? Why, have you little girls?"

"Ah! faith, that I have," he answered, smiling; "two of the bonniest that ever trod on old Ireland's green soil."

Well, that was something, after all. I had never known or played with little girls; those that I had seen in our little country churchyard on Sundays always attracted my fullest attention, their snowy aprons, glossy curls and light straw hats calling forth unbounded admiration on my part. So all the way along I dreamed of my girl cousins, and so delighted was I at the prospect of soon meeting them, that I think my great bereavement was almost forgotten; which shows how easy it is for a child's thoughts to be drawn from shade to sunshine. I was feverish with anxiety as we approached the silvery Shannon, on whose lovely banks was situated the mansion that contained the daughters of Sir Clarence, and I scarcely noticed the beauty and novelty of the scenery, although my eyes were fixed on the shining river wandering so gracefully along, bearing on its smooth surface sail boats, steamers and pleasure skiffs. At last, the postillion announced:

"Here we are, little master."

I jumped up hurriedly, thinking of my cousins, and leaped lightly from the carriage. As we alighted, two lovely little girls came running to meet us, whom I instantly knew to be my cousins. For some time my gaze was riveted upon them, trying to decide which (for the life of me I could not tell) was the lovelier. There was a striking contrast between them, which, I believe, is considered strange in the members of the same family; but nature is whimsical, and as regards the little girls, the dame was indulging in her characteristic to the fullest extent. The one on the right was tall, graceful and elegant-looking, a profusion of light hair which had escaped from a comb hung over her fair shoulders. Though I was lost in admiration of this, my oldest cousin, still there was that about her which intuitively told me that she was far from loveable or amiable. The other daughter was apparently, and as I afterwards found to be so, some years younger. She was small and active (and as I could not see their faces well, I could not decide which was the prettiest), with dark, short hair curling all over her well-shaped head.

"Where is my cousin John? Didn't he come, papa?"

"Here I am," I said, advancing and extending my hand, which was warmly clasped with her little ones.

"I am so glad to see you," she continued. "I feared you would change your mind and wouldn't come at all. Do you think you will like to live here?"

"I will like to live with you," I answered, "but I don't think I will like her," pointing to the other sister, who had gone on with her father.

"Oh, don't say that; you will like my sister Eleanor. She is so beautiful the servants all call her Queen Eleanor, and she is so elegant that papa is quite proud of her."

"Isn't he proud of you, too?" I asked; "I know she is not so pretty as you are."

"Oh, yes she is! I am so little and good for nothing. Papa kisses me sometimes, and calls me his little dark Italian, but Eleanor is so much handsomer and smarter that papa lets her stay more with him and tells me to run and play."

"What is your name?" I asked, as I saw for the first time her soft, brown eyes, which a baby would have noticed for their loveliness. "Is your name as pretty as you are?"

"Oh! do you think I am pretty? Everyone loves to be called pretty; but then you won't say I am pretty when you see my sister Eleanor, and then she is a real young lady, sixteen, and I'm only twelve; and look here, you must not make Eleanor angry, for she won't like you if you do. She is papa's English beauty, so she says."

"And does he not call you his beauty, too?" I asked, wondering how he could think anything lovelier than the little brown-eyed girl that was bewitching me.

"No, he just calls me Nita, that's my name, you know."

"No, I didn't know; but it's very pretty, but not sweet enough for you. Why don't they call you something beautiful, something that would suit you?"

"Oh, I think my name suits me exactly, but you call me as many sweet names as you please in papa's stead. But look how late it's getting, and papa and Eleanor are at the house by this time" (for we had been standing still since our conversation began), "come, let's run," and catching me by the hand, she darted off like a young antelope, and I found myself out of breath before I knew it.

"Oh!" she said, laughing, "you are tired already, and your face is right red from running. Why, you ain't half as smart as I am. Now just see if you can keep up with me. Here I go," and suiting the action to the word, she sprang off like an arrow, nor did she stop till she was fairly seated on the steps of the mansion.

I felt really ashamed, being beaten by a little girl not as old as myself, and would have seated myself under one of the trees, but she called me, saying: "Come here, John, and sit by me. You are angry with me, and I am sorry, but then, you know, you are smarter than I am in every other way but running. I am no bigger than a sparrow, and fly instead of run; but we must not get angry with each other, for that won't be nice."

"No, indeed," I answered, "I couldn't get angry with you, and everything you do is right." I was about to add more, when looking up I saw Eleanor. I thought I had never seen such haughtiness, but she was very beautiful.

"Is that our cousin?" she asked, "that ugly thing? What a nice time we'll have showing him off!"

"Hush! oh, hush! Eleanor," said the little girl, starting up, " don't say that, please, don't; John is a real nice, good boy."

"And *beautiful!*" scornfully replied the other, with a toss of her stately head; "we will be quite proud of him, no doubt."

"As proud of me as I'll ever be of you," I said, angerly; "don't think I'll ever call upon you to show me off. I will be just as anxious to keep out of your way as you will out of mine; and as beautiful as you imagine yourself to be, Nita is a thousand times lovelier than you'll ever be with all your beautiful dressing;" for, child as I was, I had noticed that Eleanor was both becomingly and handsomely dressed, whilst her little sister wore only a plain pink gingham without decoration or ornament.

"You are an impudent, ill-bred boy," she cried, flushing with anger, "to dare to speak to me in that manner. You had better remember, you little beggar, what you say in future."

"*Little beggar!*" I said, rising and advancing towards her; "you call me a beggar? why, I could buy and sell you, and do you think I am afraid of you or what you say?"

She stamped her foot with rage, but seeing my determined, unflinching stand, she took her little sister by the hand, saying: "You shall never again play with this young savage," and walked away, taking the little girl with her.

And this is how I first met my cousins. One of them I had already learned to love, for her sweetness, amiability, and free, easy manners had attracted me irresistibly towards her. The other I scorned, disliked, and felt that I almost hated, though I thought her very beautiful; still, she was so repulsive that I felt I could never feel a friendship for her. I was still thinking of them, and wondering if I must enter the house, when I heard my cousin Clarence ordering a servant "to hunt me up and bring me to him, for I must be hungry." The kind manner in which the order was given brought tears to my eyes, and by the time the servant reached me I was sobbing bitterly.

"What! crying, honey?" asked the old man, as he took my hand; "there, there, darlint, dry your eyes and come to your supper, and you'll be all the better for it."

"I don't want any supper," I cried, "just let me sit here."

"I know you feel very lonesome, my little boy, and sorrowful, too; but come to your supper, child, or the master won't like it."

I allowed him to take my hand and lead me away into the dining-room. I was completely dazed by the brightness of the silver-plate and the gaudy colors on the delicate china. I felt like a fish out of water when I seated myself; even the beautiful lamps attracted me with the figures of wood nymphs wreathing fern leaves to place on their graceful heads. The pictures, too, were magnificent and richly colored, and I noticed particularly the richly carved side-board with its marble top. I was so busy looking at all this splendor that I forgot the presence of the family at the table until little Nita, who had moved her chair close to me, said: "Do eat, do eat something, Johnnie; I know you must be hungry, now, are you not?" and she placed a hot light roll on my plate.

"Yes, I am right hungry," and was soon feasting on the good things with which my cousin Clarence's table was plentifully supplied, though there Eleanor sat, my *vis-a-vis*, looking haughtier and more scornful than ever, and doing everything but positively making faces at me. On her right sat another lady, whom Nita informed me was Eleanor's French governess, "and they like each other very much," she continued, "and you ought not to make an enemy of her, for it would be so disagreeable for you." Nita was not allowed to say much during meal times, so, when Sir Clarence made the sign to depart, she rose hurriedly, stole her little hand into mine and whispered, "Come, now; I will show you all my pets." Away we went, first to the dog kennel, where the lazy quadrupeds were sleeping away, but, on our near approach, grumbled and growled until they recognized their young mistress, when they jumped and fairly danced for joy at the very sight of her. After we had given them their supper, we walked to see the birds, who had their pretty heads tucked away under their wings and too fast asleep to mind our approach. So onward we went, from one thing to another, till the bell summoned us to retire, and the first kiss that was ever imprinted on my lips by a little girl was pressed there that night, and I went to sleep and dreamed of it.

CHAPTER IV.

JOHN MAKES A DISCOVERY.

WAS very soon like one of the family in my cousin's house, doing pretty much as I pleased, being the only boy, and not a very naughty one, as I heard Sir Clarence say one day. This speech flattered me to such an extent, that I made every exertion to appear to the best advantage.

Little Nita was my constant companion, and never did little boy and little girl get along so well together. Our leisure hours were employed catching fish from the silvery Shannon, playing hide and seek, making soap bubbles which were borne upon the air, reflecting the rays of the sun in their seven glorious colors, and in every other amusement which childish fancy could think of or dictate.

I do not think that Eleanor was pleased at our happiness. She would often pass us in our sports, cast upon us a look of supreme contempt, and go on without uttering a word. We tried to avoid her as much as possible. I never liked her, but, for Nita's sake, always treated her respectfully, though at times it was very hard to do so, when I saw the rude, rough manner in which she treated her little sister. Often I would be on the point of breaking out into a reproach, when a look of appeal from Nita would hush me instantly.

I one day made a discovery when I had been at my cousin's for six or eight months, which equally surprised and pleased me. The servant Patrick had been busy all the morning dusting the magnificent pictures in the drawing-room; before, I had only cast a careless eye around on these beautiful paintings which were hung there; but on this particular morning I was more attentive in my inspection, and found myself examining them very closely. Amongst them were two handsome portraits, which hung directly opposite each other. I did not at the time analyze the feeling which attracted me so closely to them. I seemed drawn irresistibly. I remember of thinking it strange that I admired them so much more than the many fancy pictures which surrounded them, and which, being more brilliant in coloring, were more apt to strike a child's fancy. Try to prevent it as I would, I would find my gaze returning to the portraits. One represented a young lady whose dress betokened the rank of an English Countess. She was half reclining upon a silken couch, the white, soft arm supporting a head which was small, well-shaped, and beautiful. Light curls were falling gracefully over, though not concealing, her snowy, dimpled shoulders. On a small table near by stood a Parian marble vase filled with roses, modest violets, white jessamine, and delicately-fringed honey-suckles. The whole picture was striking and very beautiful. I turned from it though but half satisfied; not that I did not think it lovely, but because I noticed a resemblance to some one whom I had seen, and was annoyed that I could not remember who it was. At length giving up in despair, I crossed the immense room to the other painting, which was well placed, having the advantage of light. It represented, also, a lady, whose dress had somewhat the appearance of an Italian peasant. The face was extremely youthful, and though not so delicately chiseled as the face of the opposite lady, still it was more endearing and expressive, claimed more of your attention, and you were captivated at once by the amiable sweetness and gentleness of the expression, which the artist seemed to have copied exactly. She was seated upon the ground, with her face slightly lifted, supported by the left hand, whose arm rested upon the trunk of an old ash tree. Instead of the peasant's hat, a scarf of deep rose color was twined in and out through the dark hair. At her feet lay dozing a great, shaggy Newfoundland dog, with a piece of light blue ribbon tied round his neck, whilst in the background curved and flowed a little brook, on whose margin grew in magnificent disorder numberless wild hyacinths, pretty water lilies, slender little blue-bells, and fancy-painted primroses. If I was worried by the resemblance to some one in the other picture, I was deeply annoyed here. I gazed and wondered again and again who it was, or what it was in this picture that was so like something or some one I had seen before. I turned away at last and left the room, but all day, and even in my dreams that night, thought of the two portraits. So, on the next morning, bright and early, I rose, dressed quickly, and stole softly down stairs into the parlor. But again I was foiled. Being tired standing, I took a chair and seated myself a short distance from the Italian girl, and was so intent examining the face that I did not hear a light footstep on the carpet, or feel that any one was near, till I felt a warm breath on my cheek, and turning, found Nita, with her large brown eyes fixed upon the portrait. I started up, looked from the picture to the little girl, and not till then did I discover the resemblance.

"Nita, was that your mother?" I asked.

"Hush, hush," she said, evidently much startled, and looking hurriedly around, "papa may hear you. Come away. I hear some one coming."

"Well, what if there is?" I answered pettishly.

"Oh! a great, great deal. Come," and taking my hand anxiously and nervously she led me from the room into the yard.

"Now, tell me," I said, "why have you acted so curiously? That must be your mother, for you are exactly like her."

"Yes, John, that is my mother, but do not let papa know I ever told you. He does not want me to know, and one evening I heard old Patrick say that little Nita's mother was a much lovelier person in every way than Lady Eleanor's. I ran to papa and asked if Eleanor and I were not sisters? 'To be sure you are, you foolish child. Go away and never come to me again with such a silly question.' I saw he was very much annoyed, and when I was leaving him he called me back and said: 'What made you ask me that, child?' I told him what I had heard Patrick say. You know when papa gets angry he gets very angry, and I always feel frightened. So, when he told me if ever I listened to servants' talk again he would chastise me severely, I went away and cried myself to sleep near the old summer-house, where Patrick picked me up, and said I was a poor neglected little girl, and that my rich sister would have a good deal to answer for."

As Nita could tell me no more about her parentage, I determined to seek old Patrick and find out from him all I could, for never had I been so interested before. After seeking some time, I found the old man cleaning out the fishing-boat on the bank of the river.

"Good morning, Patrick. How are you this morning?"

"O, so so, young masther," he answered, looking pleased at my salutation.

"Are you going fishing?" I asked. "If so, do let me go with you. I have nothing to do to-day, and am crazy for a fish."

"Well, well," he answered, "I reckon you must go, and see what luck you'll have; and I am sure I'll be glad enough to have ye with me too."

"O, now, that's the way to speak, Patrick. When you confer a favor it is so much nicer to do it as if you were receiving one. Don't you think so?"

"Ah, faith, that it is, young masther. It's no use doin' a kind thing unless you can do it in a kind way."

After a few more careless remarks, we found ourselves launched fairly out on the sparkling waters and hauling in the bright fish in surprising quantities. After we had completely exhausted ourselves with our work, we leaned lazily back to enjoy the bright sunshine and surrounding scenery. I was growing anxious, as I hardly knew with what success my questions would meet, and over and over again, in my mind, I asked myself how I would broach the subject. But at length my desire to know the truth overcame everything else, and I determined to begin.

"Well, Patrick, tell me all about my cousin Clarence, and all about Eleanor and Nita's mothers. Wasn't Sir Clarence married twice? Now, Patrick," I continued, seeing him drop the oars and look at me astounded, "you see I have some knowledge of the family's history, but it is very limited; so you must give me the information I want. Eleanor and Nita are not full sisters. This I know. Now, you must tell me the rest, and why it is kept so secret that even Nita is afraid to say that that pretty Italian girl is her mother's portrait."

"Who was so busy," began the old servant, between vexation and astonishment, "who, I say, was so very busy as to furnish ye with the secrets of the family?"

"Nobody," I answered coolly. "I acquainted myself with the better part—at least I guessed—and it was afterwards acknowledged to me that I was right."

"Well, did anybody ever hear the like of it?" went on the old man, splashing the oar excitedly in the water. "To think of a boy only fourteen years old finding out what has been kept secret in the family for thirteen years, not even a servant, myself excepted, knowin' a word of this, nor even the young ladies. Well, well, what is the world coming to?"

"Coming to an end," I said, composedly, knowing I had the old man in my power, and, in self-defence, he would have to acquaint me with the whole secret before we turned our faces homeward.

"How did ye find out anything about this?" he asked, after a few moments' pause.

I told him the whole circumstance, and after a few more questions, got the following:

"My present masther was the second son of the Earl of Graham, and of a wealthy and noble English family. The first time I met Sir Clarence, he was somewhere about two-and-twenty. He was mighty handsome, and both polite and courteous in his manners. I do not think he was much of a favorite with his father, for I remember when I was first taken into the service of the family, I heard the old Earl remark that that Irish boy (meaning me, of coorse) would be a very able valet for Clarence, but that Sir Edward should have Bretainge, for he was an able servant (a smart young Frenchman who lived in the house), and his oldest son could not and should not put up with the inconvaniences arising from having incompetent servants. And from that time I was assigned to Sir Clarence, and never have I regretted that it was to him that I was given, for he was much a finer man in every respect than his older brother.

"When my masther was about twenty-six, there figured in London one season a rich young Countess, Lady Mary Carlton. She was considered both beautiful and fascinating, but unlucky was the day when my poor young masther first saw her; for she, like most of the young ladies of her time, fell very much in love with him, and he, poor fellow, was soon caught. A marriage was the consequence, of coorse. But, oh! what an unhappy one it was! for Lady Mary was only beautiful in face, and even when that was angered it was dreadful to look upon it. My poor young masther soon found 'that it's not all gold that glitters,' and he said to me one evening (for in me he always confided), after a scene in which my Lady figured conspicuously, 'Patrick, I wish one of us was dead; for this life I cannot endure much longer.' My heart bled for him, but there was no help for it.

"After little Eleanor was born, I thought there would be a change. But no, no; it was worse than ever. She could not bear for the father to caress his own child, so great was her jealousy. I will not enter into the details of the next three years, at the end of which an epidemic entering London took away the 'fiery Countess,' as I always called her.

"After her death, my masther traveled a great deal through France, Germany, Spain, and Italy. In Italy we lingered longest, Sir Clarence examining and admiring the great masters, Murillo, Raphael, Vandyke, Angelo, and all those others whose names I have long since forgotten. I never shall forget the evening we arrived at Naples, where the sky was as clear and blue as a sapphire in a lady's ring, and the waters of the bay, stretching out far and wide, as smooth and unruffled as the surface of a polished mirror. Ah, it was a lovely scene; and great Vesuvius off in the distance, puffing up its black smoke, seemingly so disturbed, forming a strange contrast to the peaceful scenery around. We lingered there many days. My masther, who was charmed, seemed unwilling to tear himself away. But at last he appointed a day, and our minds were made up to start at that time.

"'Only five days more to stay in this charming place,' my masther said one evening. 'Arnt you sorry, Patrick?'

"'Indade, I am that, sir,' I answered; 'but, I suppose, you would like to see your little girl?' (We had left little Eleanor with relatives in England.)

"'Yes,' he said, very anxiously. 'Poor little thing, I wonder how she is getting along?'

"My masther was always a fond father.

"'I think,' he said, in a few moments after, 'we shall pay a last visit to Vesuvius this evening, Patrick.'

"It was calm and beautiful as we wondered forth, and we trod on flowers at nearly every step whose fragrance rose sweetly upon the evening air. The Neapolitans always tell you to 'go to the Mountain,' as they call Vesuvius, and the country at the foot of this mountain is most fertile and cultivated, and favored in every way by nature. We stopped to rest before ascending. I leaned upon a small cane that I carried in my hand, whilst my masther walked around to admire the beautiful spot. I was watching his manly figure walking about, when a very soft voice at my side caused me to turn, and a little Neapolitan girl, with a basket filled with beautiful flowers, asked me to buy. I was gazing with deepest admiration on her lovely face as my masther came up. On seeing the stranger, I noticed that he was more attracted by her beauty than I ever saw him struck by anything before. She held her flowers towards him, and asked in the same soft tones 'if he would buy them?' Sir Clarence kindly took the flowers, and then made her sit down and tell her simple story,

"'She was a little orphan,' she said, 'living with an aunt, who had a large family, and was only tolerated on account of the pitiful sum she made selling flowers; and if a certain amount was not sold every day, she was severely chastised on her return home in the evening.'

"Sir Clarence was deeply affected by this short but sad history, and true it is, that 'pity is akin to love,' for, before leaving Naples, he made this poor little orphan his lawful wife—his 'child wife,' as he used to call her, for she was only fifteen.

"We didn't return to England immediately. My masther was, I think, ashamed of his hasty marriage, though I know he loved and dearly loved this pretty creature. But pride is a bad thing, and my masther has his full share of it. I was almost thankful that the sweet, gentle little Neapolitan did not live to learn that her husband, whom she almost idolized, was ashamed of her. Ah, no! for she closed forever her soft, brown eyes one mild evening, in Venice, and the only legacy she bequeathed was little Nita, who is her mother's image and has her mother's loving disposition. Sir Clarence left for England at once, but remained there only a short time; came on here, bringing his two little daughters, and has forbidden his second marriage being mentioned for fear the little girls should find out that they are not full sisters. My masther's life has been a very romantic one, you see," wound up the old man, as he drew our little boat to shore and gave up fishing for the day.

CHAPTER V.

JOHN FALLS INTO DISGRACE.

HAD promised old Patrick to relate nothing of what he had told me, "for," said he, "the young lady knows nothing of this, and as she is not of the amiable kind, it is better that she should be kept in ignorance. It is very different with Nita; she would love Lady Eleanor all the same—kind, warm-hearted child that she is." And, indeed, old Patrick was right. Never was there a more tender, affectionate little being—and cheerful, bright and beautiful. There were many clouds, too, around her young life, for she was very lonely and evidently much neglected. Her father rarely or ever smiled upon her or spoke one kind word. I know that he was a loving father, but he was so completely ruled by his oldest daughter, whom he admired most extravagantly, that he had come to believe that Nita was an inferior little girl, caring for nothing but dolls, kittens and pets of every description; that she possessed no talents, little mind and little character. Whilst Eleanor, on the contrary, at her sister's age, was fluently reading German, French, Spanish and Latin, and had both refinement and character, and was not, like Nita, fond of living in the kitchen with the servants, making boon companions of the gardener's and lodge keeper's daughters. No, indeed; she was very different and he was glad her tastes differed from her sister's. "Of course," he thought, "what else could I expect;

she inherits all this from her plebeian mother. I might have known that it would be impossible to refine her. She will never make a decent entry into society, never. Oh! if she were only like her sister. What a superb girl Eleanor is, with so much good taste, exquisite penetration, and so dignified and stately. I have just reason to be proud of her, and for having her for my companion, for she imbibes all my fancies and tastes thoroughly—a fine girl, a fine girl."

But whilst Sir Clarence was thinking all this, why did he not think also, that it was owing to his neglect and his oldest daughter's statements that his younger child appeared to such disadvantage. She was neither inferior nor weak-minded. On the contrary, she was high-toned, with chaste and beautiful tastes, a highly-gifted mind and bright and striking ideas combined with much simplicity, generosity and gentleness of nature, which bore a striking contrast, and which was very agreeable to the haughtiness, amounting to rudeness, and imperiousness of Eleanor.

One evening, a circumstance occurred which appeared propitious to Nita's future happiness; but, unhappily, favorable circumstances to-day may be counteracted by unfavorable ones to-morrow. On this particular evening, Nita and I were flying kites in the yard and playing about as usual. She was in a most gleeful humor, and seemed, by her exuberance of spirits, to have infused her cheerfulness and gaiety into me, for never did I feel so full of fun and pleasure. I had given her kite a lift on a strong breeze which had just sprang up, and called to her to run and see how it would sail on the air like a huge bird. She sprang off instantly, and her little light feet seemed fairly to fly as she ran through the yard with the flying kite. I tried to keep up with her, but might as well have tried to keep up with the young antelope, and I had to stop for breath. Being near the steps of the balcony, I seated myself to admire her swiftness and graceful little form; a slight noise caused me to look around, and I saw Sir Clarence, Eleanor and the French governess watching Nita also. I saw by the expression of Sir Clarence's face that he was admiring his little daughter.

"I declare, now," he at length said, "she's as graceful as a gazelle. Why, her feet scarcely touch the ground. But, ah! there, the string has broken. Poor little fairy, how disconsolate she looks. She is scarcely larger than a humming bird, she is so tiny."

At this point, Nita came running up, and stooped to pick up a little guinea pig which her father had given her some days before, and to which she seemed devotedly attached. As she was about to seat herself beside me, with the guinea hugged tightly to her breast, her father leaned towards her, and said:

"Are you tired, little girl?"

"A little bit, papa," she answered, laughing, going up to him; "Did you see my kite?"

Here Eleanor interposed:

"Why, papa, one would think you never saw a kite fly before. I'm sure it's very easy to do."

"Oh, yes, yes, daughter," he answered, "it's easy enough, I know. How is the little guinea coming on?" turning to Nita.

She was about to answer when Eleanor said: "Give me the little guinea. I haven't played with it for a long time."

Nita, without a word, placed it in her arms. She commenced, instantly, to teaze the poor thing, and handled it so roughly, that it struck its sharp teeth deep into the soft flesh on her bare arm. In a fit of rage, she caught the tiny creature and threw it with such force against a marble pillar close by, that it fell upon the marble floor, gave two or three faint moans, while one or two convulsions passed over its little body, and then lay quiet and dead.

A cry of pain burst from Nita's white lips, while the tears streamed from her beautiful eyes.

"Ah, my poor little guinea! my poor little guinea! Sister Eleanor, why did you do it? Ah! papa, is it really dead? Look! look!"

"Yes, my child,', he answered, half sorrowfully, taking her hand; "yes, it is dead, but papa will give you another one very soon."

Turning to Eleanor, he said:

"You have pained me very much, my daughter, by giving way to your temper in such an unlady-like manner. Try, hereafter, to have more control over yourself." He then stooped and kissed Nita's forehead and drew her away with him. I followed, and we bent our steps towards the river. During the rest of the evening, Sir Clarence devoted himself to us, shared in our amusements, related the most wonderful tales for our entertainment, and altogether we had a most charming time. Nita was inexpressibly happy.

Never before had her father displayed such demonstrations of affection for her, his neglected little girl. When the bell rang that night for us to retire, my cousin kissed his younger child in a tender, fatherly manner, calling her his little darling, and asked God to bless her. Me, also, he kissed in a kind, caressing way, bidding me be a good boy and to get up early, and we would all three go fishing on the river in the morning. I left his study, in which we had been lately sitting, and, boy-like, went bounding up stairs to my chamber. Just as I was about to lay my hand on the knob of the door, I felt a soft touch on my shoulder, and Nita whispered, "Oh, Johnnie, I'm so happy." Then, kissing my cheek, she ran off hurriedly in an ecstacy of joy, and I, big, foolish boy, went to bed and wept with happiness at the good fortune of the little girl whom I so dearly loved. And this good fortune and excessive happiness lasted only for *one short week*, during which time Sir Clarence had us with him constantly. He played ball with us and took us long walks through the fields, told us marvelous tales of fairies, genii, dwarfs and hobgoblins, rode with us on our ponies, and in all our sports he was partaker. During these short seven days Eleanor was the most miserable person I ever knew. She trembled for fear Nita would rival her in her father's love. There was another motive, too. Eleanor was both selfish and covetous, and the presents which Sir Clarence gave to his young daughter during that week were looked upon by her with the greatest envy; and day after day she wondered how she could, with her wiles and artifices, misrepresent the child to her father. One week from the day on which the guinea pig was killed our joy was turned into sorrow. After our dinner hour Nita and I had a long recreation, and this evening we were to spend it in playing battle-door and shuttle-cock. We were in the long drawing-room and our game was a brisk and lively one. "Now we are at a hundred," said Nita, "let's see how many we can make."

"One hundred and twenty-five" she had just called out, when the door opened and Eleanor entered. The sudden entrance so surprised Nita that, instead of throwing the shuttle-cock back to me, she threw it unintentionally at her sister and struck her a hard blow over the eye. A young tigress in a rage could not have shown more temper, which, if possible, was increased as she caught a glimpse of herself in the large mirror opposite, which showed her that the delicate white lid was swollen and purple, and in a fair way of spoiling her beauty. She rushed forward with clenched fist, and struck little Nita's face until the blood entirely forsook it, and it was as white and blanched as a water lily.

"I did not do it intentionally, Eleanor," cried the child, lifting her hand to avoid the blows; "indeed I did not. Pray, stop!" but these gentle expostulations only seemed to increase the fury of the beauty. If any man or boy, with the soul of either, could stand and see such injustice practised upon a little being whom he dearly loved, they could stand more than I could or wished to. And if I did come of a cool, calculating, phlegmatic race, I could be as hasty and impulsive as other people. And as I saw the way Nita was treated my hands and arms seemed acted upon by a dozen electrical machines, which increased in force as I rushed towards Eleanor, and, as quick as lightning, she was measuring her length upon the floor, while I, the next minute, was hugging and kissing little Nita, begging her not to spoil her pretty eyes crying, and that all the Eleanors in the world should not injure one hair of her dear head as long as I was living.

A violent shake of my arm here brought me to myself, and turning around, to my dismay, I faced Sir Clarence.

"Well, young man," he began, his voice trembling with passion, "this is nice behavior for my ward to be guilty of; how dare you lay hands upon my daughter, and treat her in that barbarous manner? I am surprised and shocked as well as insulted and offended, and—"

"Papa," said Eleanor, rising and going to her father's side, before he finished his sentence; "papa, John was not the whole cause of this; look what Nita has done" (showing her swollen eye), "she did this, and purposely, too; she threw the shuttle-cock directly at me, and this is the result."

"You know, Eleanor," interrupted the child, sobbing, "you know I did not do it intentionally; indeed I did not. John, was it not an accident?"

"Yes, it was," I answered, "and she knows it was, too."

"Say no more, John," said Sir Clarence, looking at me in great anger; "don't say a word. Your conduct, sir, is shameful, and in no way to be excused. You have displeased me beyond measure."

"And you, Miss Nita, have behaved quite as badly as your cousin. You should be ashamed of yourself. See what you have made your sister suffer. I never heard of such conduct and such unlady-like behavior."

"But, father," cried the child, "I did not hit Eleanor purposely; I really did not. I could not help the way the shuttle-cock flew."

"Papa, I say it was not accidental; she hit me purposely. I was watching them playing through the window, and they had kept up the game ever so many hundred without missing till I came in; then I was made a target, instantly, and Nita and John pretend to say it was accidental."

"Well, well, my daughter," began Sir Clarence, "they will both pay for this, for I am displeased, very much displeased, indeed. Here, Mademoiselle Marie," addressing the French governess of the little girl, "take this pupil of yours and lock her up in the small room in the third story; she is to remain there till bedtime without supper. I wish to be strictly obeyed," he continued, as he saw something like reluctance in the kind woman's face, "I wish and will be, you understand, Mademoiselle?"

The woman bowed, and taking Nita's hand, left the room.

"Now," said Sir Clarence, turning to me, "go to my study and wait there till I come."

"Certainly," thought I, as I found myself seated by the window of the room where no one entered but the master, "certainly, he doesn't think to treat me as a child? I wonder what he will say?"

I had little time for reflection, for in a very few minutes Sir Clarence entered. He drew a chair near me, and, after a few minutes silence, began a lecture which I hope will never be inflicted upon any other poor boy. After this, I was sent to undergo the same punishment as poor little Nita.

"Well," thought I, as the servant turned the lock and left me a prisoner, "well, if Nita only knew that I, too, was under lock and key she would feel better, for 'misery loves company.'" As I was thus musing, and wondering in what apartment the child could be, I heard a low, choked sob from the next room. I went straight to the keyhold and listened. Again I heard another. "Nita!" I whispered, putting my mouth to the keyhole; "Nita! are you there?" but no answer. "Nita!" I said, in a louder voice, "come here, if you are there;" but again no answer. "It is only I, only John." I heard a soft movement and a few light footsteps, and the little girl's eye was peeping at me. "Oh, John, are you there? what made them lock you up, you were not to blame? I'm so sorry, and glad, too, for I was afraid to think of being here to-night alone, but you being there will keep my spirits up."

"Yes, keep in good spirits," I returned, "for I will tell you a story and we won't mind being locked up." So down we sat, she in one room and I in the other, both in disgrace, but both of us happy for all that, for she was naturally cheerful, and soon forgot her troubles; and I was happy when she was.

CHAPTER VI.

JOHN IS FULL GROWN.

I DO not intend to linger over Nita's and my childhood, though it was by far the happiest portion of my long, weary life. I was a happy, joyous boy then, but now a sad, sorrowful man. I could, if I did not have compassion on my readers, relate event after event of pleasure which happened in my boyhood to little Nita and myself. There were, too, hours of sadness and disgrace for both of us; but our troubles were of short duration, for if we were locked up for some trivial offense, which was frequently the case, since Eleanor never tired of misrepresenting us, just allow us to peep at each other through the keyhole or some window and we were happy, and took our punishment with the best possible grace.

I am very much afraid, my friends, by the time you have read to this chapter, you will have become very tired of the joys and sorrows of two children, and will have said with much irritation, "I do wish John and Nita would grow up. We have had quite enough of them." So, in compliment to you, though it is with a "feeling akin to pain," I pass over a period of seven years, which made me a man and Nita a woman, and, oh! such a fair graceful woman. Her light figure had lost none of that ease and swiftness of motion, blended with the most perfect grace, that was peculiar to her alone; and her lovely eyes, so soft and expressive, literally spoke every emotion of her heart. It would be folly for me to say that there were none as lovely as Nita. I do not intend going so far. She was lovelier than any one else in the world to me, though others differed from me very often. She was, however, admired extravagantly and loved by all, and thought much more attractive and winning, although not as beautiful as Lady Eleanor. I once heard an English Countess remark that she would willingly give her rich estates for Nita Graham's eyes, and did she but possess them, she could and would make the whole world bow before her; and on the same evening, a gentleman said to me: "That little cousin of yours is exceedingly lovely, though one must know her before he can fully appreciate her beauty. Her face, at first, does not strike you as being so beautiful as Lady Eleanor's, but after a few moments' conversation you quite change your mind. I never saw eyes that so mirrored one's heart." And such remarks I was continually hearing. Eleanor took good care that Nita should see as little of society as possible when her vanity allowed her to notice the effect she produced.

But the time came at length when Nita must make her appearance in public.

"Nita is quite old enough," Sir Clarence remarked, when the question was discussed, "and a very sweet, pretty little girl she is, too. Yes, she must make her *debut* this fall; that's settled."

When her father spoke so positively, Eleanor could only pout her pretty lips and remain silent. I think I mentioned that Eleanor inherited a large estate at her mother's death, which brought her annually a large income. But this great amount was scarcely sufficient to satisfy her demands. Poor Nita never saw a cent of it, and was dependant upon her father's generosity for the little ornaments she owned. One evening I overheard her remark to her waiting-maid:

"I'm sure, Charlotte, when I do go to Lady A——'s ball (this was to be Nita's ball) I will feel mighty shabby. I won't look at all like a nobleman's daughter, and Madam Blanche seems to think my wardrobe quite good enough for me. Why, I have not a suitable set of jewelry even, and I wouldn't ask papa, for he has been so generous to me lately that I fear he would think my wants will never be supplied. I am sure I will feel very badly. 'But what can't be cured must be endured,'" and she commenced humming an air, seeming to forget in an instant her difficulties.

I went down stairs muttering, "Oh, this is the way, is it? Well, it shan't be so always."

I had a call to London a week before the ball on pressing business. After my engagement was concluded, I found myself in the great city with nothing to do but to think of Nita. And as I walked down the busy streets, I remembered that I had heard her speak of not having a suitable set of jewelry for the ball. My eyes wandered from store to store, until at length I saw the one I most wished for. I entered; the brightest gems were before my eyes; for a time I was almost dazzled by the brilliancy of the precious stones; but finally remembering how limited my stay was to be, I chose a set of beautiful emeralds which I thought would be acceptable to Nita, and shortly after bade adieu to Merry England and was sailing across the Channel.

I found Nita, on my arrival, in the conservatory, watering a row of Nile lilies which she claimed as her especial property. She did not hear my footsteps, and my arms were around her before she was aware of my presence.

"Oh, I am so glad, so very glad, you have come, John! I have been real lonesome. You don't know what a difference your absence makes. It don't seem like home without you."

A thrill of exquisite joy passed through me at these words, and as I saw truth written in every lineament of her lovely face, my heart throbbed with a pleasure that I never felt before.

"And you really missed me, Nita? Why, I didn't think you would notice my absence."

"Oh, you old hoax," she answered, laughing, "you know very well I missed you. Aint you just as good as you can be, and who thinks of giving me one moment's pleasure but you?"

She turned away her head to hide a tear that was glistening on her cheek, as she felt the truth of these last words.

"After awhile, Nita, you won't think so much of me. You will be in other company, and there will be new scenes and new faces to divert you, whilst I'll be here alone, sadly wishing that the time had never come when others could give you pleasure and when you would not look to me for every enjoyment."

"What do you mean?" she said, very much startled, "Am I going anywhere that I won't be with you?"

"No," I answered, "but you are going into fashionable society, where you will be flattered and caressed, and by some loved; but there will be others, Nita, who will frown upon you, and jealousies will arise that will make your life almost unbearable; but then, again, there will be an excitement which you will relish and which you will not be willing to relinquish for the quiet joys of home."

"Why," she answered, smiling, "you speak most gloomily of this life that I am doomed to lead. I'm sure it will not be so dreadful. Speak more cheeringly for pity sake, or I will despair of ever having a peaceful moment."

"Oh, I trust it won't be quite as bad as that; but experience is the best of masters."

We had been walking while we were speaking, and had entered the parlor just as I had finished my last speech.

"Now," I said, "give me one more little ballad while we are here alone, for next week you will be little with me, and whilst you are away will forget how dearly I love to hear you sing."

"I will never forget either your likes or dislikes," she answered, as she seated herself at the instrument and began a low, simple melody.

When she had finished, she turned to me and said:

"John, how can you say that I will forget you? you who have ever been my best friend. You know my life would have been a poor, lonely one if it had not been for you; and you to say I will forget you! I never can or will."

"Neither have I forgotten you, my little cousin," I said, as I laid the sparkling jewels before her. "This you will accept as a little token of my remembrance."

"O! are these for me?" lifting the beautiful stones from the soft velvet and looking at them more closely. "Oh, these are lovely, magnificent! John, did you get these for me? and did you think of me whilst you were in old, bustling London?"

"Indeed, I did—there and everywhere."

"Well, what shall I say to thank you?" she asked, looking up into my eyes.

"Not a word," stooping and kissing the blushing cheek, "not a word; only wear them for my sake at Countess A——'s ball."

"Yes, indeed, that I shall; but you ask little return for such a superb present. I want to do more for you. What shall it be?"

"That is all I ask now, dear Nita," I answered, "though perhaps in the future I shall be more extravagant in my requests."

"You are a dear, dear cousin," she whispered, "and you can never ask too much of me or more than I will be willing to do," and throwing her arms around my neck in the old childish way, she told me again that I was her dearest friend.

Oh, if I could only have claimed her then! But no, no. It was ordained otherwise, and I try to believe that it was for the best, and that our Creator knoweth what is for our good, and dealeth most mercifully with even the weakest of His children. My conscience would not allow me to tell her then of all my love. "No," it said, "don't be selfish; let her see something of the world; do not injure her now by exacting a promise that she will be yours; you may be very sorry if you do, for she loves you only as a brother. Wait." "Yes, yes," I said, with a sigh, which attracted her attention.

"Why, John, you are sighing, whilst I am so happy. Why, what is the matter?"

"Here, while I am with you, dear Nita, you are sufficient for my happiness."

"O, you old flatterer, to say such a thing! You dear old flatterer," she repeated, laughing. "But I havn't seen how becoming my jewels are. Now, look while I put them on, and see if I am not pretty. Don't laugh, for I want to look dignified. Oh, are they not becoming!" she said, as she caught them up to her bright, young face and glanced in the large mirror opposite. "Won't I eclipse everybody?" she went on playfully, "and don't you think some one will fall in love with me, and perhaps, too, John, might marry me? Then, I wonder if papa would feel just a little sorry when he should not see little Nita about the house, though he does think me such a trouble? And Eleanor, maybe, would be repentant for not letting papa love me as much as he does her. You are the only one that I know would be sorry," coming up to me and laying her hand on my arm, "and my greatest regret would be to leave you, John."

I turned away and left the room, for the bare thought of losing her sent a bitter sorrow to my heart's core.

CHAPTER VII.

NITA'S DEBUT.

THE long looked for, and much talked of, night of the ball at length arrived, when Nita was to make her debut. For the whole day preceding it, everything was in the utmost confusion. I could not catch a glimpse of the young lady till towards evening, when I was fortunate enough to see her long enough to ask what dress she would wear on the great occasion. "Oh! the dress papa gave me—white silk with your emeralds, do you think I will look pretty?"

"Lovely!" I said, in return.

"Well, good-bye, until you see me looking so," she answered, as she ran lightly away, "then you can pay me as many compliments as you please, for I will have time to listen."

In the evening, at half-past nine, we were to start for Countess A's, where a large and select party were invited to receive Nita. It was quite dark when the two girls came down to get into the carriage. I noticed that Nita, though I could not see her face, was sad and very silent. I did not ask the cause, thinking perhaps that the novelty of the occasion alarmed her, and, without having spoken half a dozen words, we arrived at the Countess', where introductions, and little ceremonies too numerous to mention, were gone through with. My two cousins, on the arms of my Lords, whose names I have long since forgotten, were ushered into the great hall. Murmurs of admiration greeted these lovely girls on every side, and their entirely different styles attracted universal attention. I soon saw my little Nita in the gay dance, with a crowd of admirers flocking around her. I was hurt and vexed when I saw that my present was discarded, for she did not wear the jewels I had thought so much of, and which would have made her look so attractive. Whilst wondering why this was, I accidentally caught sight of them in a brilliant blaze of light on the neck and arms of Eleanor; and how beautiful they were, and how lovely they made her appear. I had never seen her half so lovely as she was this night. I was so much worried for a while, that I ceased to look towards either of my cousins, and tried to forget them entirely, as I saw they had no need of a faithful watcher. I soon left the crowded hall and went to one of the verandas, and seating myself, thought of the injustice practised upon me by Nita. I felt it very keenly, and was fast making myself very miserable, when I was touched on my arm. Looking up, I saw a young gentleman, who, in his hurry, forgot to introduce himself, but who seemed to be well acquainted with me.

"Mr. Meredith, please introduce me to your younger cousin, she is so bewitchingly beautiful."

"If you will honor me with your name, sir, I will do so," I answered, coldly.

"Oh, I beg you will excuse me," he answered, "your lovely relative has made me quite forget my politeness. Arriving after your party, I was denied the pleasure of being one of the first who were introduced."

Pleased with the address of this young man, I arose instantly after hearing his name, and accompanied him to the dancing saloon. I found Nita with several gentlemen who were all requesting the pleasure of a set with her. She saw me advancing, and came forward a few steps to meet me. I introduced Sir Charles Stuart, and in a few moments left him talking to Nita in a manner which was altogether very prepossessing and attractive. I went back again to my lonely seat on the veranda, continuing my dispiriting wondering why Nita should have treated me thus, and thinking of the handsome young Scotchman I had just presented to her. All seemed so dark to me then, that with a weary yearning, I longed for my boyhood to come again, when she was all my own. I shuddered as I looked to the future, and felt what it had in store for me. As I sat thus musing, Nita and Sir Charles passed out and joined a throng of promenaders on the balcony. A thrill of jealousy shot through me, and when I saw by the moonlight the bright, lustrous eyes looking into his, and the soft smile wreathing her lips, I determined to bear it no longer. Remembering that my cousin had warned me not to stay out late, but to let common sense make me come early, I looked at my watch, and finding it long after midnight, started to seek Eleanor, to suggest to her that we had better leave. Of course, she was the one to say Yes or No to our going. I found her almost alone, and was pleased to see by her tired look that she would be willing to depart. She had not received the usual amount of attention that was generally allotted her, the "little sister" having already begun to eclipse her. "Where is Nita?" she asked; "call her, if you please, and we will go." This was soon done, for I did not like to see Nita with this gentleman. I felt a presentiment of coming evil when I thought of those two together. We were not long in preparing and were soon on our way home. Nita talked all the time of how charmingly she spent the evening, and of Sir Stuart, and told us that she had promised to allow him to visit her. This was a new pain, for I was very jealous of this Sir Charles, whose gentlemanly manners and agreeable appearance were so striking. I had only known him two or three hours, and was, in truth, obliged to acknowledge that he was the most attractive gentleman I had ever met.

"What did you think of him, Eleanor?"

"I did not have the pleasure of an introduction, but as you seem to think so, I suppose he must be overpoweringly fascinating."

Soon after this scornful speech, we reached home, and, for the first time since I had come to live under my cousin's roof, I retired to my chamber without kissing Nita good night. In a little while Sir Clarence came in to learn the events of the evening. I told him all about the ball, and could not help mentioning that Nita had discarded the jewels she had promised to wear, and that they were very becoming to Eleanor.

No doubt he saw that I was deeply hurt, for at the breakfast table, next morning, after telling his younger child how proud he was of her (all parents are proud of their children if by the world admired, and so it was with my cousin), asked;

"What did my little Italian wear that made her so captivating?"

Eleanor had always managed it so that Sir Clarence should be blind to Nita's many charms; how she did this, I never knew, but, strange to say, it was true. My cousin seemed to be under the impression that Nita was admired by no one, but this ball had the effect of opening his eyes.

"What did I wear, papa? Why, of course, the beautiful white silk you gave me, and your pretty bracelets."

"Was that all the jewelry? You were certainly modest."

"No," she said, blushing, and evidently much embarrassed, "I wore a set of corals."

"Why," asked Sir Clarence, rather severely, "did you not wear the set of emeralds that John was kind enough to give you?"

"Because," she stammered, and then stopped.

"Because, what?" persisted the father.

I saw then what he meant, and felt sorry for her, and remarked that I supposed that Nita thought they were more becoming to Eleanor than to herself, and was too unselfish not to allow her to wear them. I saw the blood start into Eleanor's naturally pale face as I said this, and she gave me one of her old looks, which used to alarm me when I was a boy, and I saw that she was very much frightened for fear her father would think that she had been capable of a mean action and that her sister was so generous. Her father, noticing this silent confession, said:

"Why did you not let Nita wear her own jewels, Eleanor?"

"Why, papa, I didn't think they would be as becoming as the set of corals. You have already heard how much she was admired, and I think it was owing altogether to my good taste in lending her the coral set."

"Well, then," I said, anxious to get my mind relieved, "Eleanor, you just took Nita's jewels and put your's in their place without saying anything?"

"Yes, I did," she answered, pettishly; "is it any of your business, sir?"

"None, whatever," I replied; "only you put me in mind of an anecdote I heard once, of a man who had his valise marked with the eight of clubs, and another man came along with the nine and took it."

She said no more, for her father was present, and before him she was always amiable. We were silent during the rest of the meal, Sir Clarence asking only a few questions relative to the ball. After we had risen from the table, I asked Nita what the programme was for the day.

"Oh," she answered, "a nice row on the river, and a soiree at Lady C's this evening. Oh! I think it will be delightful, and John," she added, blushingly, "isn't Sir Charles charming?"

I could scarcely bear to hear this man praised in my presence, and answering "Yes," hurriedly ran into the hall, where I encountered Eleanor tying on her hat, making ready for the sail.

"John, of course you are going to pilot us?" she said, as I was passing on.

"It is very likely I will not, Eleanor. I have business to attend to which I think will prevent me; business always before pleasure, you know." So I staid at home, thinking how miserable my life was becoming, and wondering why did girls become women, and why didn't we always stay children. I was wondering all this, when Patrick, who was dusting the furniture in my room, turned to me, and asked:

"Were you the person, Masther, who introduced my young Misthress Nita to Sir Charles Stuart?"

"Yes," I said, looking at him in surprise, "why do you ask?"

"Because," he began, "Sir Clarence is very much put out about it; he had no idea, I heard him say to Miss Eleanor, that it was this Sir Charles you mentioned last evening. There seems that there has been some misunderstandin' between Sir Clarence and this Stuart family, and, whatever it was, Sir Clarence is seriously displeased."

This raised my spirits wonderfully. I felt like a new man. Perhaps, after all, I was indulging in imaginary trouble that would never be realized. I arose, whistling, with a lighter heart than I had had since Nita's debut was first spoken of. I met my cousin on the landing.

"I was looking for you to tell you of the great mistake you made last night in introducing Nita to a Stuart. They are the bitterest enemies of my family, and now I am forced to see this Sir Charles escorting my daughter about, visiting my house, and obliged by the rules of etiquette to treat him like a gentleman, when it would be more acceptable for me to see a woolly-headed African about me."

"I am sure Sir Charles" (feeling sorry for him when I heard him unjustly spoken of) "is quite a gentleman, and I never have seen a more fascinating one."

"Fascinating! That is just it," he said, interrupting me. "We will have Nita fascinated with him presently, and then we will have nice acting."

"God forbid," I murmured to myself, and left the excited old man to calm himself. Sir Clarence's words were prophetic, for every day I was convinced that she was more and more enamored of this young stranger, although she had been told of her father's objection to him. This dislike on Sir Clarence's part did not seem a sufficient reason for her refusing to give him her love. I heard afterwards that it was a very little thing which had made the breech between the two families.

One day when a party of equestrians had returned from their ride, Nita being amongst them, I saw Sir Charles, as he lifted her from the saddle, place a tiny white rose-bud in her hand, and whisper, "With the emblem." She blushed deeply as she received it, and I saw her kiss it in such a tender manner on her way to her room, that my heart ached with jealousy. But this was only one of the "trifles that was confirmation strong as proofs of holy writ," for every day they happened, and every day I felt hope dying within me, and knew that I was becoming a sadder man.

"I have something to say to you, John," she whispered one evening after tea, laying her hand on my arm. "Come out into the summer-house. I cannot tell you here."

We went out together, and after we were seated, she said:

"I am almost afraid to tell you for fear the flowers will run in with the news to papa."

I knew what it was, but said nothing.

"I must tell you though," she continued. "I would die if I did not tell some one, and there is no one will advise me as you can."

I still sat silent, and she went on.

"Why don't you ask me, John? Have you no curiosity?"

"I know what it is, Nita," I at length said; "I know what it is. You are engaged to Sir Charles Stuart."

After this there was a pause for some time. After awhile she raised her eyes to mine and said:

"And you, too, are angry with me. I knew papa would be; Eleanor is not interested enough in me to care one way or the other; but for you to be angry and not to advise me—oh, John, John, it's more than I can bear."

Here she broke down and burst into tears.

"My darling," I cried, "I am not angry; don't think it. What am I to do? How am I to advise you against your father? for you know he will be—well! I may say furious. Can I tell you to be disobedient?"

"Oh, John," she sobbed, "what am I to do? I

cannot give up Sir Charles. It would break my heart to be obliged to be separated from him for ever. And he, too, would feel it so keenly!"

Yes, I knew he would suffer, for it did not take me long to know that this young Scotchman fairly worshiped this girl.

After a long silence she spoke again:

"John, you will do all you can for me, won't you? Oh, pray do, for the love of mercy. You can make papa become reconciled. Do, John, do. You know you are the only friend I have. Oh, you *will* help me. Say you will, my cousin."

"My dear, kind cousin, *yes*," I answered.

And this was all that I could ever be to her—*her friend, her cousin*—and she should never know how this friend, this cousin, loved her! No! better that my heart should break in silence with this great sorrow than to give another pang to her gentle heart.

I walked alone in the dim starlight after she had left me, feeling as if these contending passions would drive me mad. I knew that I could stop Sir Charles from ever coming to the house again. All I need do was to make known to Sir Clarence what I had just heard and agree with him in disapproving of it. Then Nita would be forever separated from this man, who stood between me and all that this world had of happiness for me. And she would naturally turn to her only friend for consolation, and I felt that, in sympathizing and condoling with her, I could gradually endear myself to her in such a manner that I would become necessary to her, and that then, discovering my deep,

deep love, she would be all to me that I desired, and (went on the tempter) do you not owe this to Sir Clarence? Remember all that he has done for you since he brought you, a lonely little orphan, to his home, where he has shielded and sheltered you from every harm. And you know what you heard him say to Eleanor, when she had told him that she thought you were getting too fond of Nita—" That there was not a man, young or old, in England, Ireland, or Scotland, whom he so thoroughly appreciated, whose advice he would sooner take, or who he would rather have for a son-in-law than John Meredith." Oh! the temptation was strong. Would I do this and secure my own happiness and save my cousin further annoyance about this young man? or would I use my influence in favor of Sir Charles? It was a hard, bitter struggle, and I walked on and on, with the stars twinkling, twinkling, but giving none of their brightness to me until right had conquered and I had resolved to plead for Nita and give her to the man she loved. I thanked God then that He had saved me from myself; and now that I am an old man in the twilight of life, I thank Him again that He vouchsafed to me the grace not to yield to my first and greatest temptation.

CHAPTER VIII.

NITA MAKES HER CHOICE.

AFTER this the days crept slowly enough. A dark heavy cloud seemed to have lowered over us all, which affected Nita very seriously. I had spoken to Sir Clarence, and told him of Nita's preference, and how worthily I thought it was bestowed; but all I could say would get from him but the permission for the young lovers to see each other occasionally; more than this he declared should never be; and when I tried to convince him that he was both hard and unjust to these young people, he hushed me with a cold rebuke, and very unceremoniously dismissed me from his presence. But as days passed on, and I saw Nita's cheek grow pale and thin, her light step heavy, and her large, lustrous eyes lose their brightness, my conscience reproached me, and I feared that I had not done all for her that I could. I was becoming very scrupulous on this point, and determined that I would fight a hard fight in her interest. What hurt me most was that she seemed to avoid me and all the family. I had seen less of her in the last two weeks than I had done for years. I could hardly stand this. I loved her so that I would rather suffer anything than she should suspect me of not befriending her. Sometimes, in passing her chamber at night, I would hear her, in soft tones, supplicating mercy from on high. One evening I was walking with my fishing-rod on the banks of the Shannon, and as usual was trying to forget myself and soften the burthen that was upon me. I had walked some distance to where two or three large willows hung their huge branches over the bright waters. Underneath their cool shade I thought to rest and refresh myself from the burning rays of the afternoon sun In the act of doing so I was stopped by the notes of a guitar, accompanied by Nita's low, musical voice, invoking the Blessed Virgin in the evening hymn. I stood where the drooping branches concealed me from view, but where I could see her, with her soft eyes raised supplicatingly to Heaven and those pure notes bursting forth from her lips. I thought I had never seen a more attractive or beautiful picture. After the hymn ceased, she leaned forward, with her chin resting on her hand, and looked pensively over the waters. How much she was like the portrait of her mother then! I was half afraid of approaching her for fear of being repulsed, and as I stood thoughtfully studying whether to advance or not, I saw Sir Charles, with his rod and line, perhaps like myself seeking, by wandering along the river, to lighten his grief. He soon saw Nita, though she was entirely unconscious of his presence. He stopped, as I had done, to gaze upon the lovely picture, and, like me, was completely enraptured. The pure love he had for the woman sitting there beamed forth from his expressive countenance and shone in his dark gray eyes. He came up and sat down by her. She started and gave a cry of joyous recognition. How I stood that half hour and looked at those two I never could tell, though I have asked myself again and

6*

again. Had I thought of myself I would have gone away, but I thought of nothing but of the lovers before me and of what I heard them say.

"Oh, Charles, is it you?" she spoke. "Have you come to hear how sad I am?"

"Then there is no good news? You need not answer, love, for I see it in your eyes. Oh! why is it that our cup of bitterness must be so full? But I will not give you up," he continued. "Never! never! Sir Clarence will and must yield at last. He cannot hold out always. And why should he visit the sins of our forefathers upon us—you, his beloved child, and I who have never done him harm, save to love his daughter so much, more than life? Oh! Nita, Nita, what must we do?"

"I don't know, Charles," she answered in tones in which grief was visible; "I don't know. I suppose I will die some day, and then they will feel sorry that they did not grant the only wish of my heart. Oh, Charles, they have never loved me as you do."

"*They!*" "*They!*" Then I, of course, was included—I that would have willingly laid down my life to have made her happy. But still she included me with the rest. I made a solemn vow then and there that she should marry this man, no matter what it cost me —and she continued. "I will never marry anyone but you, Charles; they cannot make me do that, and I can never love anyone again."

"My beloved," he cried, kissing passionately the little white hand he held so firmly, "you shall never belong to anyone else. *Never!* I would rather see those sweet brown eyes closed forever more than know that they would look with love in another face; they must be *mine! mine* to look at and grow cheerful in their brightness; *mine,* when the cold world has dealt hard with me, as it ever does with all its children, to cast away the clouds that will hover over me; *mine* through life, and *mine* after, I trust, in a blissful eternity."

"Yes, always yours," she murmured; "always, always."

I turned away, then, very sad and lonely, and went back and sat upon the veranda, waiting, waiting, waiting, for what? I hardly knew. At last Nita came; the rose was then upon her cheek and the brightness in her eyes. After all, the meeting must have been a joyous and happy one, though they were like children groping in the dark, not knowing where they were going or what they would do next. I rose as she came and went to her.

"Nita," I said, "will you come with me? I would like to speak to you."

"Is it of importance?" she asked; "if not, I would rather you would put it off until to-morrow, as I wish to go to my room now."

"As you like," I answered, and turned away in search of Sir Clarence, and found him in his study hard at work on some papers.

"I wish you would come here and help, John. I am up to my eyes in work, and don't know what I shall do unless you lend me your valuable assistance."

I was soon at work with him, and we were not long

in righting and putting up the papers. After we had finished, I looked at Sir Clarence and saw that he was in an excellent humor, and felt that this was the time to speak.

"Sir Clarence," I began, "I wish to speak to you once more on the subject I broached the other day, and I trust you will hear me through. Are you prepared to listen?"

He nodded assent, and I began:

"I have come to plead in Nita's behalf. She is your child, Sir Clarence, and you are wrecking her happiness. Don't you see every day the roses paling on her cheeks, and see that she never indulges in one of her old merry laughs? You cannot but know that she is very much changed for the worse, and that change is caused by you. Will you still persist in making her miserable, and perhaps send her down to an early grave? For Nita is a woman that loves truly and tenderly. She is not *cold English*, but *warm-hearted Italian*. I think that every parent should establish his child's happiness when it is within his reach. And the question arises now: Will you, Sir Clarence, make your child happy or cause her young heart to break through an unjust prejudice? For there is no man more to be admired than this Sir Charles, and if you would view this matter from an impartial point, you would see at once how wrong it was to visit the doings of their forefathers upon this young couple."

He did not interrupt me whilst I was speaking, but looked out the window at the trees, which were nodding their branches to and fro in the gentle summer breeze.

I glanced at him and saw that he was not unmoved. The tears were in his large blue eyes, and he was winking fast and hard to keep them in their place. After an uncomfortable pause, he turned abruptly to me and said:

"Why is it that you plead for Nita? Are you so very anxious to get rid of her?"

Anxious to get rid of her! Was I anxious to tear the sunshine from my heart? Anxious to turn day into everlasting night?

"No, Sir Clarence," I said when I could master my feelings, "I am only anxious for her happiness, and I believe that this is the only way it can be obtained."

"Well, then," he answered, "if she loves this Scotchman better than her silvery-headed father, let her go with him, but she is never to come back to me again. Tell her this, and tell her that she can have her marriage here, where you and Eleanor can witness it. But after that, she goes. Not another word, John Meredith. It is you that are sending my child away from me. Take my message to her, and tell her to decide between her lover and her father."

It was useless to say more then, so I left him to look for Nita. I found her with Eleanor, which was something strange, something that had not happened for months, I may say years, that these two sisters should have a confidential talk together. I begged pardon for intruding upon them, and asked Nita if I could see her when she had finished.

"We have finished now," said Eleanor, rising, and I noticed that she had quite a satisfied look upon her face, and spoke more cordially than was usual with her.

When I had opened the door for Eleanor to leave, I crossed the room to Nita and said:

"I have something of importance to say to you, little cousin, which I fear will have to commence with a confession on my part, and in accusing myself I am afraid I will appear very badly in your eyes. This morning, I was an eaves-dropper for a time, when you and Sir Charles were on the beach. I hope you are not angry and do not think me very dishonorable, for the instant I recollected myself I departed. Since then I have had a conversation with Sir Clarence."

"And told him all about it, I suppose," she exclaimed, springing up and casting a look of reproach upon me.

"I had hoped, Nita," I replied, "that in all these long years you would have known me better. I had no desire, no reason, no thought, to make your meeting known to your father."

"Forgive me," she said, with tears in her eyes. "I was too hasty. It would have been so unkind for you to have told papa. But I ought to have known you would not."

"No, I would not," I answered, hurt to the quick, "though I spoke to your father of you, and he told me to tell you that you could marry Sir Charles——"

"Oh! did he!" interrupting me, and throwing her arms round my neck in the old, old way. "Oh, John, you dear, dear cousin! You did this for me, and I have been so unkind to you lately."

I took her arms from my neck and walked away a few steps, and then came back to her and said:

"Nita, you leap to conclusions. Your father will not allow you after you marry Sir Charles to come back to him or to his home again. He told me to tell you to choose forever between Sir Charles and himself."

She was touched and grieved, but answered promptly:

"I have chosen, John. I will take Sir Charles. Eleanor has said that she thought it ridiculous in me to hesitate at all, and that if she was in my place she would have married him long ago."

"Did she? And she has been advising you?"

"Oh, no," she answered, hurriedly, "not advising me. She only told me what she would have done had she been in my place."

"Very well, Nita. Then I suppose you have decided and it's all settled?"

"Yes, John, it's all settled, and the sooner we are married the better it will be for all of us, I think. Perhaps papa will feel more lenient towards us when we are absent, and not visit his resentment upon poor Sir Charles and myself. You will never forget me, John, will you? When I am far away you must think sometimes of me, as I will often of you, my more than cousin, my *brother*."

"I trust, my dear Nita," I said, interrupting her, "that you will remember me as your brother, and a very fond one too; and in trouble or in want, if you should ever be in either, think of me as one who will be but too eager to assist you. Now, don't forget this. As I loved you as a little boy, I love now, and I always will."

She sat down as I spoke and covered her face with

her hands to hide the tears that were chasing each other down her face. I smoothed her soft tresses, and tried to soothe her as best I could.

"Oh, John, I have been so unkind to you in the last few days. Will you try to forget it and forgive me, for I am truly repentant? You are the last person in all the world whom I would willingly offend. I love you too dearly. And we will be friends when apart, will we not? And when I write to you you will answer sometimes, and tell me all about my poor dear papa, yourself, and how my old home looks, which I am doomed never to see again."

Here she completely broke down, and fearing that she would make herself ill by indulging in her grief, I took her from the place and spent the rest of the evening in endeavoring to cheer her and to divert her mind from the painful separation which was so soon to take place.

CHAPTER IX.

JOHN AND ELEANOR MEET WITH AN ADVENTURE.

THE marriage day came at last. Sir Clarence never left his study during the week before but to come to his meals, which were eaten in silence by all. Even the servants felt the grief which precedes the departure of the loved one. We could not see that she would ever again come back to us. Had the grave opened to receive her we could not have felt it more painfully; and still she was going and of her own free will. Oh, Love! what a mystery thou art, and what sacrifices are made for thee. Here was a young girl, with the strongest natural attachments, with a father she almost worshiped, with a home that was endeared to her by a thousand tender associations, willing, nay happy, to forego them all for a stranger she had scarce known three months. I did not close my eyes the night before the day which was to take all that was dearest in this world from me forever. I sat by the window and watched the stars as they rose, twinkled and sparkled, and then I saw them slowly fade away before the bright rays of morn.

The day, in the forenoon, was bright and cheering. The marriage was not to take place till the evening, and the couple were to cross the Shannon at a point nearly opposite and go direct to Scotland, which was to be Nita's adopted country. As the last star had passed away, and the sun in all his brilliant majesty rose upon the world, I left the window, by which I had been sitting so long, and went out into the garden to refresh my mind, and to try to summon the courage to witness the marriage without betraying myself. I came upon Nita suddenly in a bend in one of the walks, where she had come, she said, "to say good-bye to the flowers and to the trees," which, in the faint morning breeze, seemed gently to return her parting salutation.

We took a quiet walk together, she the while talking of her marriage and looking happy and miserable by turns. She could not endure the thought of her father not witnessing the ceremony. This was a cruel blow. I think she would have been supremely happy had he blessed her nuptials; but the pain she suffered at the idea of his not being present was real happiness to what came afterwards. We were called to an earlier breakfast than usual, the servants desiring this that they might spend as much of the day as possible with their beloved Mistress; and Sir Clarence was a man that never refused a reasonable request. It seemed scarce an hour between morning and evening, so rapidly did the time fly which was to rob poor me and all the household of our darling, and cast a dark shadow over our lives which years might lighten but never could remove. I felt as though some horrible nightmare had possession of me, and how I managed to give her away (which sad privilege devolved upon me), and listened in silence to her plighting her vows to another man, I never could tell. Some invisible power seemed to be holding me up and encouraging me to go on to the bitter end. It was all soon over—it took only a few minutes to separate her life from mine. She turned to me pale and trembling, and as I took her in my arms and kissed her, she whispered:

"I wonder if papa will tell me good-bye, John? Oh, if he only would! if he would kiss me and tell me that he is not so angry I would be so very, very happy. Come with me, and I'll try, anyhow."

I saw that she was flushed with hope, and hoped, too, that when Sir Clarence saw her he would forgive. I opened the door softly for her to enter, and saw her father, with his face buried in his hands, leaning upon the table. He did not hear us enter, and started with astonishment when Nita laid her hand upon his bowed head, and whispered:

"Forgive me, papa, and tell your poor child good-bye. Oh! dear father, tell me good-bye and bless me before I go."

She looked so fondly and so pleadingly into his eyes that I had no other thought than that he would forgive, and would not banish this gentle child forever from his home, but was sadly startled when he rose from his chair, with an expression of countenance that I never saw Sir Clarence wear before, and said, in a voice husky with passion:

"Go!" pointing to the door, "you are no longer a child of mine! You forfeited that claim when you became the wife of Sir Charles Stuart. Go!" he repeated, opening the door by which she stood, paralyzed with fear and disappointment, "and remember what your cousin, I suppose, has told you, that my house is no longer a shelter for you, and that you leave it immediately, to return on no pretence whatever."

I dared not look towards the poor child to whom he had spoken so rudely, but as I heard a low cry of pain escape her, I attempted to interfere.

"Sir Clarence, you surely will not part from—"

Here he stopped me, saying:

"Sir, when I wish advice from you I will ask for it, otherwise, you will be pleased to remain silent." Then, turning to Nita: "Be assured, Madam, I will not depart one iota from what I have just said. You have made your choice, abide by it; and again, *I command you to go!*"

Knowing it was useless to parley with him further, and thinking, too, that he might only make the wound deeper in the poor young heart should I attempt a reconciliation, for Sir Clarence would not stop at anything when made angry, I took Nita's hand, and led her through that door and from that room which she was never to enter again. I saw them to the sailing vessel which was to take them to the opposite shore, I waved an adieu to her as she sat by Sir Charles' side, with the moonlight kissing her sad, white face, I watched the little vessel skim lightly over the silvery waters, and until the last white sail grew dim in the moonlight, and then turned with a sickening heart to that lonely future which was to be mine, and to that old home of hers which would now look sad and gloomy to me for many a long day. This night, like the night before, I spent by my window without closing my eyes. I never can tell how those two nights passed without making a crazy man of me; but God suits the back to the burden, and I thank Him for leaving me my mind, health and strength during that bitter trial. For weeks I don't think any of us came to see each other. After our meals, which were eaten in silence, I would go away from everybody. I wanted to be alone, and Sir Clarence and Eleanor's presence was a positive pain to me; particularly was this the case when I would allow myself to think about the many acts of injustice done by them to the young, gentle girl who had passed forever out of our lives.

One evening, about a month after Nita's marriage, Eleanor came to me as I was reading in the library. "John," she said, "do put up that stupid, old book and make yourself agreeable, for once in your life, to me. When Nita was here I never expected a civil word from you, but now that she is gone, it will fall to your lot to amuse me at times. So, come now, and don't look as if you had lost your wits; let us take a sail, a ride, or anything of the sort to break up the *ennui* of our lives at present. I do wish papa did not require me to stay at home so closely. What good does it do? I'm sure I'm not sorry that Nita is married. I think it is the best day's work she ever did, for, I dare say, if she had not taken Sir Charles she never would have been married."

"Well, Eleanor," I answered, "commence, now, and make up your mind to be an old maid, for if that was Nita's only chance, I fear you will not have one at all."

"Oh, that is just like you, John Meredeth! taking

Nita's part always, and being as uncivil to me as you possibly can."

"The cap seems to fit you exactly, but I would try and not make it a disagreeable one."

"Why didn't you tell me at once that you did not intend making yourself agreeable to me, and that I may go about my business, for I see that you want to do so?" she said, reddening.

"But I don't intend telling you any such thing, Eleanor, and am completely at your service."

"Well, pray, do come, then, and let us go where I asked. I think a ride will be the very thing for us, for I want to try my new pony, and it's the very evening for a ride on horseback."

We were not long in preparing and were soon cantering over the smooth country road, and talking more to each other than we had ever done at any one time in our lives before. "I think my pony is perfectly delightful," Eleanor was saying, when we had ridden about a mile, "and he doesn't seem to be scary in the least." The words were scarcely out of her mouth when my young horse, who was at times quite unmanageable, got frightened at a little peasant boy, who was throwing stones, and jumped and reared at such a rate that it was an impossibility to quiet him, though I used every exertion in my power to do so, and I was considered an excellent horseman, but all my efforts in this case failed, and I was thrown with such violence that I became, for a while, insensible. Eleanor's young pony took affright and ran off. I knew nothing of this, until returning to consciousness, I found she was not

with me and that there was no trace of her to be seen.
My own horse was standing near, quietly grazing on
some fresh green grass which the summer rains caused
to spring up all along the side of the hard road. I
soon had possession of him again and was hurrying at
an almost frantic rate trying to find poor Eleanor, whom
I feared was killed or very badly hurt, when a little girl,
who I saw through the rails of a cottage fence, told me
me that the young lady's horse had run off in that
direction, pointing to the left, over a rich green meadow, where some careless persons had left the fence
down. I rode as rapidly as my horse could go, fearing all the time to come up with the poor girl, lest my
worst apprehensions should be realized. I looked all
over the large meadow but could see no one. At the
opposite side to where I was I noticed a grove of oaks;
to that I directed my animal. In a few moments I had
almost reached it, and saw Eleanor's pony at the further end of the grove tied to one of the trees. This
gave me some hope. I jumped off my horse, tied him
in like manner, and began my search. It was not long
until I caught sight of a man, on a little rustic bench
near by, stooping over a form which I knew at once
must be her's. I ran quickly forward, in my anxiety
and fear; the gentleman turned, as I advanced, and I
saw by the expression of his face that he was very
much troubled. I sprang forward and looked at Eleanor. She was perfectly unconscious, but not, I thanked
God, dead as I had expected.

The gentleman had one of her white arms in his
hand, from which the crimson blood was slowly oozing

—he had been thoughtful enough to bleed her when he found her insensible.

"I am truly thankful to you, sir," I said, addressing him, "for your thoughtfulness and kindness in this unhappy affair. I was thrown myself just before this young lady's horse ran off, and was unconscious of the occurrence when it happened."

"I assure you," he replied, in a very courteous manner, "that I am not deserving of thanks, for I consider it a great privilege to be allowed to serve so beautiful a creature," pointing to Eleanor, who was still insensible. "I saw the whole occurrence—your fall, too, which was a very severe one—and would have helped you had not this young lady's horse started off. I followed her immediately, but it was impossible for me to get to her before she was thrown, though I trust she is not badly hurt and that we may hope for a speedy recovery."

"God grant it!" I answered, while bathing her temples and face with cool, clear water which flowed in a little stream near the grove. I soon had the happiness of seeing her open her eyes. I leaned over her and asked "if she felt any pain."

"No," she said; "but, John, wasn't it dreadful? I was sure that I was going to be killed. Wasn't it horrid in your old horse to get frightened? my pony never moved, and would not have run off if you had not been thrown. Just think," shuddering, "how near I was to death. Oh, it frightens me so to think of it! Oh, it was horrible! horrible! John, don't it frighten you, too?"

"Of course, it does; but you must thank this kind gentleman, here," beckoning him to me, "he has, I think, saved your life, Eleanor."

"Let me thank him, then," she cried, rising. She thought, as she told me afterwards, that it was some poor Irishman whom I wished her to thank for saving her life, and when she saw a dignified, stylish-looking stranger, she was so taken by surprise that she could scarcely thank him at all.

"I hope you are not suffering any, my Lady," said the gentleman, in the polished, courteous manner I before noticed. "Your fall seemed very severe, and I feared would be a serious one. I am truly happy that my fears seem not to be well founded."

"I am not suffering at all, and am most truly thankful to you, kind sir," said she, "for your timely assistance. I should like above all things to know the name of the gentleman to whom I am so indebted."

He bowed gracefully, and introduced himself as Lord Gordon. We were no less courteous than he, and, in a few minutes, we were all chatting away like old acquaintances under the oaks. Eleanor quite revived, and used all her arts and charms to captivate the English Lord, for such he told us he was. I leaned with my head against one of the great trees, thrown back as far as it could be, for it seemed to be ready to burst from the effects of my fall, and putting in a word now and then only to let them know that I was thinking of them, but wishing, with all my heart, that I was resting on my couch at home. Eleanor, after all, was not so badly hurt as myself, and now, recalling the adventure after these many years, it seems strange that we both should have met with the same accident, and that it ended so differently for us, which you will hear as I proceed.

"I am afraid," said Eleanor, "that my pony may play the same trick again. Indeed, John, I am afraid really to ride him and your horse is no better. What shall we do?"

"If you are able to walk to yonder house," pointing to a little white cottage near the end of the meadow.

"Oh! I know I could not walk there," interrupting me. "I could never do it. Why, just look how far it is!"

"Well, what then will you do, Eleanor?" I asked. "I must go and have the carriage sent for you, and it is too late for you to stay out here any longer."

"Will Lady Eleanor accept of my steed?" said Lord Gordon, seeing our dilemma. "He is as gentle as a lamb, and I am sure will partake of his master's feelings, and not behave so naughtily as your little pony, which, I think, I can manage."

"I feel that I can never sufficiently thank you, my Lord, for all that you have done for me this evening, and I accept your kind offer willingly and gratefully," said Eleanor, in her softest, sweetest tones.

"I beg that you will not refer to this any more, my Lady, for I do assure you that nothing gives me as much pleasure as to be of service to you."

After a few more complimentary speeches on both sides, we were fairly started. Gordon accompanied us to the residence of Sir Clarence, who met us as we rode up the avenue, and who seemed greatly surprised at seeing a stranger with us and Eleanor on a strange horse.

I rode quickly up to him to tell him of the events of the evening before the others came up.

"Sir Clarence," I said, "Eleanor and myself met with an accident whilst riding. We were both thrown from our horses, and this gentleman has very kindly assisted us."

"Here, papa, thank Lord Gordon for saving your child's life," said Eleanor, riding up, "for which I know you are grateful," she continued, laughing, and kissing him as he received her into his arms.

"Let me first thank God and His Blessed Mother that you are safe, my child," said Sir Clarence with some agitation, "and then I will thank this kind gentleman and hear how it all happened." He paused for a few moments and uncovered his head whilst he made his thanksgiving, and we all involuntarily bowed also in humble acknowledgment of the great favor vouchsafed us from on high, and of the goodness and patience of our Heavenly Father to his poor, weak, erring children. Sir Clarence then gave Lord Gordon his hand, thanked him in a most cordial manner, and insisted upon his remaining under his always hospitable roof during the night, which I saw the gentleman was only too pleased to do. The evening passed off pleasantly enough considering the danger Eleanor and I had escaped. Eleanor played and sang several songs from the most fashionable operas, which had the effect of completely captivating the English Lord, and I was just thinking how fascinating this beautiful girl could make herself, when she suddenly stopped in the midst of a very fashionable air, and broke out into a hymn of thanksgiving to the Blessed Virgin, which was so plaintive and full of pathos, while she so sweetly acknowledged her kind protection, that tears rushed unbidden to my eyes, and Sir Clarence leaned his head on the centre table by which he was sitting and sobbed aloud. I looked towards Gordon, and remembering that this hymn was Nita's favorite (who I don't think I have mentioned was always a pious practical Catholic, whilst her father and sister were only nominal ones), and seeing that the Lord was entirely absorbed in Eleanor, I stole softly to my cousin's side and whispered:

"As your Heavenly Father is merciful, be you also merciful. As He has spared Eleanor suffering and pain, spare you Nita."

He started, but before he could speak I had left the room

CHAPTER X.

ELEANOR IS MARRIED.

ANOTHER year had passed, with its joys and its sorrows for all the world; marriage and given in marriage; the reaper death had been as busy as of yore, mowing down the young and the old; but the world went round still; the sun shone as bright in summer and as dull in winter; the flowers bloomed as sweetly in the spring and the leaves fell as lightly in the autumn, as if no vows for weal or woe had been irrevocably taken, or no souls launched into eternity to be forever happy or forever miserable. I had heard from Nita several times, her letters all breathing the deep, pure love she cherished for her husband—all telling of his many noble qualities and of his strong affection for her. She seemed very happy, loving and being beloved by him. But every cup of happiness must have its poison drop, and the one in Nita's was the continued anger of her father towards her. He still obstinately refused to become reconciled to his "erring one," as he chose to call her. He would not allow her name to be mentioned where he was, and that loved name seemed to be entirely blotted out from that old mansion, and perhaps her image from the hearts of some—for nothing is easier than to forget—but in mine her memory was as fresh as those white roses near me, which, being just freed from their crystal dew drops, are looking up to the sun in all their beauty, purity, and youth.

Eleanor had managed it so that the poor child was cut off without a farthing. She urged Nita to get married, and whilst doing so pretended to take his views of the matter, and appeared to him to be very much grieved at Nita's disobedience, as she called her marriage, when speaking to Sir Clarence. I did not find this out for some time, and directly I did so I went to my cousin to try to open his eyes to the deception that was practiced upon him. He silenced me instantly, asking me if I thought that I or any other man or woman could make him think that his child, who had chosen him before all on earth, could be capable of a meanness, and, as I knew, had all her life been respectful, dutiful, and submissive to him as it was possible for child to be. It was certainly neither my wish nor intention to prejudice this doating father against the daughter that he had such unbounded confidence in; and I believed, too, that Eleanor did love him after a fashion; but it was hard for me to keep from telling him that it was *avarice*, not *affection*, which made her apparently so loving and obedient, and that if he had been a poor man with no fortunes to bestow, he would know his daughter, whom he so idolized, to be very, very different from what he so fondly imagined. Without answering, I turned and left the study in silence, resolving that I would never marry and then I, too, would have fortunes to give away, and Nita should be the one benefited by them. What did it matter if she and her husband were poor? Was not my wealth to the last farthing at their service? And so I wrote to the dear child; but of course did not pain her by telling of what Eleanor had done or what Sir Clarence had resolved to do, but only urged her to accept a little present from me; and in the grateful note which came in answer, I saw that it was most acceptable and feared it was needful also.

She sent me about that time a small oil painting of herself—the shoulders and head—with the long dark hair, falling gracefully over her neck, looped at one side with a tiny pink rosebud, with its three green leaves. And those large, expressive eyes are now looking down upon me as it hangs over my little mantel, the only ornament in the room, and for which I would not take in exchange all the ornaments and valuables in this great world. No, no! I love it far better than all these things, nor would they even tempt me to part with it—this little picture, with its ebony and gold frame, and its sweet eyes that look at me the last thing every night and the first in the morning.

So, as I said, the year passed on as other years had gone. Eleanor and Lord Gordon had met frequently. He used to make our house his home, at Sir Clarence's urgent request, every time he came over to Ireland. Those were happy visits for Eleanor. They used to ride, sail, walk, play chess, and sing duetts together. She was very, very happy. Everything seemed to favor her, her father being scarce less captivated with Lord Gordon than herself, and it did not require a close observance to see that these two young persons were mutually in love, and that Sir Clarence approved of it. "My Lord Gordon" was considered first in everything in the whole household. I was not with them much. This affair did not have the same interest for me that the one of last year did. I cared little how it went, knowing that a disappointment in a love affair would be of no injury to Eleanor either physically or mentally, and it was the same to me whether she was out of the house or in it. Of course I wanted her to be happy, and would, were I called upon, help her in every possible way. But such a reflection was unnecessary, for I had never seen Eleanor Graham crossed in anything. She always had her own way, never was thwarted in accomplishing her ends, and all of her wishes seemed granted so instantaneously that a child fond of fairy stories would have thought they were granted by magic. She came to me one evening and said:

"Well, John, I suppose you know that I am to be married at last. Lord Gordon and I have had the happiness of knowing each other for over a year, have been in love all that time, and I think it might last a little longer as it has lasted that long. He is both handsome and rich, and quite a suitable match for me, papa thinks. What do you think of it?"

"Why, I think this, Eleanor: if you only marry Lord Gordon because he is handsome and rich and think your love will last only a little while longer, that you had better remain single; for matrimony is too sober and serious and too great a sacrament to be trifled with."

"Oh, of course, John Meredith! That is just like you! Talking like some old preacher, and looking like your last hour had come! I do wish you would not look so much like a hypocrite; it is disgusting. There is no one who will make me as happy as Lord Gordon."

"Well," I said, "I must compliment you upon a choice selection of words. But I will not quarrel with you just the week before your marriage, though I will acknowledge I feel in the humor after what you have just said. I will show my gallantry, and hold my temper."

"Yes, you had better," she returned, laughing, "for I will soon have Lord Gordon to help me, and I know we can both give you a whipping, if you are six feet."

"Very well," I said. "Whip away. It will not destroy either my spirits or my health, I think."

"No, I don't believe anything would do that, though you have looked both pale and serious ever since Nita married that poor Scotchman. But come and look at the jewels that I have just received from Paris and my elegant *trousseau*."

I am afraid I did not compliment them as highly as they deserved, for they far surpassed, in beauty and richness, anything of the kind I had ever seen before. When I would compare them to the miserable preparations for poor Nita's marriage, scarce a year ago, my tongue refused to speak the words that Eleanor was evidently expecting, and at last she left me, much displeased and disappointed.

Shortly after she left, Sir Clarence called me into his study to tell me that he had given his willing consent to Eleanor's marriage, and that she had told him that she never, never would have married without it. Of this I had my doubts, but did not utter them, and congratulated my cousin upon the pleasure Eleanor's choice seemed to give him.

The eve of the marriage day, like all days long looked for, came at last. Eleanor was all confusion and worry, giving a thousand directions. She had even me running from parlor to garret all day, fixing first one thing and then another, and everything which my hands could do, which she was pleased to consider "were much more valuable than that done by those stupid servants, who positively knew nothing."

Towards evening I went out near one of the fountains to rest, as it looked so cool and refreshing there, and because I was anxious to get rid of the hurry and bustle which was going on indoors. I had drawn a bench from between two old yews, placed near one of the marble pillars supporting the large basin that held two swans forming a fountain. I was leaning near this cool, lovely place, admiring the swans, when Eleanor came up and, seeing me, said:

"John, do you think to-morrow will be a fine day? You know there is some Irish superstition about marriage days being pretty; do look at the barometer and see how the mercury stands."

"Now, Eleanor, I would like to call you what you called me the last time we conversed upon the subject," I answered.

"Oh, but, John, in a marriage of this kind it is so necessary for everything to be propitious. You know how unpleasant it would be if it were otherwise. I am not jesting, now, and I do want you to look at the mercury and tell me what kind of a day to-morrow will be."

"It is no use looking at it just now, Eleanor; but, if it will gratify you, I will sit up until twelve to-night, and report then."

"Oh, then," she said, "I would be fast asleep, and it would matter very little if it rose or fell."

"Then I can do nothing for you except to wake you up early in the morning and tell you whether the sun is shining or not, and if it is not, send word to Lord Gordon to wait until the next fine day."

"Oh, hush making fun of us," she returned; "it is no joking matter."

"No," said I, "if I thought of it as you do, if to-morrow was a gloomy day, I would certainly send that word to Lord Gordon."

"Come," said Eleanor, suddenly changing the conversation, "come and help me tell that stupid Jackson how to arrange the flowers and vases. You know I can never do any thing unless I have some one near me to advance an idea."

"Oh! Eleanor, I am so sorry that you found me here. I was in hopes that my day's work was over, for you certainly have kept me busy, and you know 'all work and no play makes Jack a dull boy.'"

"You ought to have played all the time, then, if it would have brightened you up any," she returned, laughing.

"Oh!" I answered, "as you are trying to rob the sun of its brightness to-morrow, I am not surprised at you trying to stea away mine."

The next morning everything was as clear and bright as Eleanor, or any other very superstitious person, could have wished. She was to be married in church at half-past ten in the morning, and start immediately for Rome, traveling over all the Continent. Carriage after carriage drove up, containing the numerous invited guests, until I began to think that the large church could not seat all the witnesses of the ceremony. Eleanor looked surpassingly lovely as she leaned upon Lord Gordon's arm, pronouncing the vows to love, honor and obey. I had noticed later in the morning one small cloud in the east, scarcely larger than the palm of my hand, that was not visible when first I awoke. I was standing by one of the large open windows as the marriage ceremony commenced, and was startled and surprised at the change that had taken place in the weather, as, remembering Eleanor's superstition, I involuntarily glanced in the direction of the speck in the sky—it had grown immense in proportion and was as black as night; near the outer edge it seemed tinged with blood, and it had almost reached the sun that was nearly over the church. I felt a shudder creep over me, but still hoped that it would not shadow the sun's brilliancy, but just as the two were pronounced man and wife, it came directly over that great luminary and caused a gloom and darkness almost like an eclipse. I saw Eleanor start, shudder and grow deadly pale, but the company clustered so closely around her to congratulate her, that she had not time to think about it. Shortly after arriving at home she met me in the hall in her traveling dress, with the frightened look still upon her pale face.

"Oh! John," she said, "did you see it?"

"What, Eleanor?" I asked, looking perfectly unconscious, and trying to make her believe that I had not noticed anything.

"Oh, the cloud! the cloud!" she cried. "I am perfectly miserable. I am sure it was ominous, and, oh! wasn't it dark. I am so nervous that I can hardly walk."

And it was so. The poor thing was almost frightened to death, and could she have seen it as I did, with its tinge of blood, I am afraid she would have lost her senses with terror. Her father called her to him to say a few parting words alone, and as I saw him put his arms around her affectionately, *so affectionately*, I thought of the other child who, a short time ago, had been repulsed and so cruelly turned out of that very room, without one kind look or word to help her to say good-bye to the home she so dearly loved. Eleanor came out smiling, with a happy face; Nita had come pale and trembling, with great, bitter tears falling from those dear eyes that would never look on the old familiar spot again. Eleanor went away in a superb carriage, drawn by four magnificent greys, with servants in rich livery, and all bidding her good-bye in a happy, cheerful manner, with everything propitious to her happiness. The other poor child walked by the pale moonlight on the arm of her husband, with me, their only companiom, to see them off and to wish them well, even the servants being prohibited from saying good-bye to their beloved mistress. She went away in the quiet night, not to scenes of gaiety and splendor, but to a quiet home in Scotland, where she would help her husband earn his daily bread with her own delicate hands.

CHAPTER XI.

JOHN HAS A STRANGE DREAM.

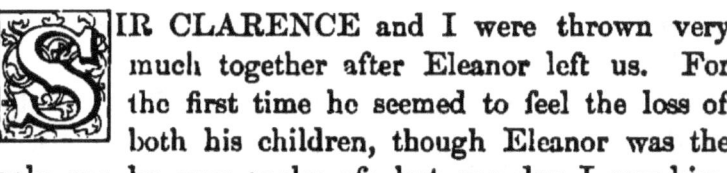IR CLARENCE and I were thrown very much together after Eleanor left us. For the first time he seemed to feel the loss of both his children, though Eleanor was the only one he ever spoke of; but one day I saw him, from the upper balcony upon which I was seated, stop before my room, the door of which was open, and gaze on the little oil painting of his younger child, and, as he turned away, the tears were in his eyes. This cheered me a little; perhaps, I thought, he may now let her come back again. I would try anyhow. But, no! when I dared to broach the subject he silenced me as before. Oh! how I would have loved to have seen that light, girlish figure walking among the flowers and the fountains, as in days gone by, and hear her calling me to help her with her roses or to twine the honeysuckle over the summer house, and hear her merry laugh ring out again. In her last letter, which had been received about a week before, she asked me if I could not sometimes come over to Scotland and see them. It was the first time she had asked me, and the very time that I felt that I could not leave Sir Clarence, who now seemed entirely dependent upon me. He had not been well all through the fall, and now that winter was coming, with its frosts and snows, I felt it would be cruel to leave him, as he would miss so much his quiet games at backgammon and chess of

which he was so fond. So the winter gave place to spring again, and in its turn, spring to summer. We had heard of two events in that time which seemed to cheer Sir Clarence—it was the arrival of two little grandsons upon the stage of life, one a Scotchman and one a little Englishman, three months being the only difference in their ages. After becoming a mother, Nita had written to me, and her letter was full of her little son, which she had baptized John Paul—John after me, and Paul after Sir Charles' father, who had been so very kind to them before his death, which took place a few months before. She finished her letter by saying that she had been married nearly three years, "which seems but a short, sweet dream, I have been so happy. If you would only come to see me, John, and see little Paul, it would be such a pleasure to me and Sir Charles. I want to see you more than anyone I know, and I want you to both know and love my child, for I feel that he will be more with you than with me. Your lives are going to be entwined with each other. You know our family are all prophetic; we seem to see everything in the future." It continued on in this strain for some time, and then spoke of Eleanor and her father with the same old love. I think Sir Clarence was hurt that Nita had given my name instead of his to her baby, but do not think he expected it after the manner in which he had treated her. He never spoke of it. Eleanor came to see us some months afterwards, bringing her little stranger, Gerald Clarence (this was Sir Clarence's full name), with her—a pale, sickly-looking creature, with two nurses, who were all the time dressing it and combing the little bit of hair that was on the top of its head into every imaginable shape, trying to make the poor little thing look pretty and attractive.

Sir Clarence, very much to my surprise, did not seem to care much for his little grandson. He would notice it sometimes to keep from hurting Eleanor's feelings, who, of course, thought it both beautiful and fascinating. I heard him tell one of the nurses one day, when she had little Gerald in his study, "Do, pray, take that baby away; I can do nothing while he is about." After Eleanor had left us, I remarked:

"I wonder if Nita's little Paul was anything like Gerald?"

"I trust not," was his answer, as he turned and left the room.

I had been thinking for a long time about Nita's letter, and wondering how I could break my going to see her to Sir Clarence, for I felt pretty sure that when I did so he would order me "never to come back again." So days spent in hesitation passed. I felt that I was necessary to Sir Clarence, who was fast growing old and infirm, and knew that if he ordered me never to return to his house my pride would not allow me to do so, and I had written so to Nita. I received another letter from her which said that Sir Charles was making an easier living than the one he had been employed at. He had purchased several small sailing vessels to convey travelers across the Lochs. She wrote: "John, I have had a real nervous fit about it, for so many dreadful accidents have happened in these Lochs, and if anything were to happen my husband *I would die.*"

One evening, four years after her marriage, I was sitting on the old veranda; it was the anniversary of her marriage night. I had thought more of her that evening than I had for over a year. It seemed as if even the drops of water from the jets in the fountains were whispering her name in the music they made, as they gently fell into the basins; and the flowers, as they bent their pretty heads of various colors towards each other, seemed talking in low tones of her who had so tenderly reared them in years gone by. A strange feeling of anxious sadness came over me as I thought again of the words in her letter—"If anything should happen my husband I would die." When I went to my room, I gazed long at her little picture. It almost seemed to take life and look at me, and smile in the old, old way. I wondered if she had changed, and fell asleep wondering if those dear eyes looked the same and if her sweet voice had lost any of its music. I cannot say how long I had slept when I started up wide awake from a horrid dream, which left me in a cold perspiration. I was not a believer in dreams, but this one seemed prophetic. I thought I had gone to see Nita in Scotland, but nowhere could I find her. I looked round the little cottage they told me was her's but she could not be found. I saw a large green meadow, full of tall waving grass, in which I wandered. While there, I noticed an old man, with long white beard and hair, holding a scythe in his hand with which he was rapidly mowing. I drew near to him and saw that in his reaping he was mowing down a beautiful white lily. I sprang forward to save it, and received the form of Nita, cold and lifeless, in my arms. I could only look at the old reaper, who answered my inquiring look by saying: "Son, the flowers must fall as well as the grass." I woke at this and a deadly terror seized me. I sprang from my bed and looked at my watch on the mantel, and found it was two o'clock. Not being able to shake off the feeling of dread that weighed upon me, I dressed and went out on the balcony to refresh myself with the night air. I lit a cigar and sat down. The moon was considerably on the wane, and the stars looked to my troubled gaze as if they did not want to give this world of ours any of their brightness. I sat and thought of the cold, dead form that had fallen into my arms in my sleep, and shuddering at the remembrance of that frightful dream—the repeater in my room had reached half-past three o'clock—when I heard in the still morning the sounds of a horse galloping rapidly over the country road; it neared the Lodge gate and then ceased. In a moment, a loud, strong haloo was borne upon the morning breeze. I saw by the light in the porter's window, which was instantly opened, that he was aroused, and his white head soon peeped through the door, followed by the necessary question, "Who comes there?"

"The bearer of a despatch for Mr. John Meredith, to be given as quickly as possible."

My heart gave a sudden bound and seemed as if bursting from my breast. Who but Nita would send me a despatch? True, I had business matters of importance in England, but would the trustees be mad enough to send a despatch to me in the night to frighten me, even if I had met with some piece of great ill-luck? No! it could not be. I was thinking all this as I ran down the stairs, for I went myself, so great was my anxiety to know what was the matter. The porter came up to me, just as I opened the door, and handed a folded paper to me. "Come in and light the gas," I said, as my hand trembled so much that I was unable to do so. I was soon standing beneath it, reading the following:

Mr. John Meredith:

Dear Sir,—I am truly sorry to have to send such painful news, but such is life, ever full of sorrow. The beloved and highly respected Sir Charles Steuart was drowned yesterday morning at 3 o'clock, whilst crossing Loch Lomond, and it is with the deepest pain that I make known to you the almost impossibility of his beautiful young wife surviving this dreadful calamity. The sudden and heavy blow seems too much for her. She asked only for you when we spoke of her friends, and begs you to come immediately.

With respect, your obedient servant,

SIR THOMAS MARSTON.

It was only necessary to read this fearful news once to take in all its terror. Those few words, "the almost impossibility of his beautiful young wife surviving this dreadful calamity," seemed stamped in indelible letters upon my heart. The old porter, who had been watching me all the time, suddenly grasped my hand, exclaiming:

"For God's sake, master, what is the matter?"

I gave a low groan as his touch recalled me to myself, and the paper fell from my hands. I pointed to it, unable to articulate a word. After reading it, he turned to me with tears streaming from his eyes, and said:

"Oh, young master, but this is a hard blow. You must go to her at once. Oh, go to her, poor thing! poor heart!" he continued, as the grief of the little girl and the graceful woman whom he had loved touched his Irish heart.

Yes, no time was to be lost. I must go, and go at once.

"Michael," I said, when I at last recovered my voice, "have my horse saddled immediately, and my valise packed—only a change; I can't wait for more—and let me be gone."

"That is right, young master," he said, and turned to obey.

I wrote a few hurried lines to Sir Clarence, and left the dispatch for him to read. I would not allow him to be called for fear it might delay me, and then, perhaps, I might never see my darling alive. I walked down to the lodge; just as my horse came up I mounted him and rode off. I was not long in wearing out my poor steed from the rapid pace at which I rode, and before I got to the relay where I could change the poor animal, he was almost fainting from exhaustion. Early the next morning I was in the sailing vessel which was to take me over to Scotland. The motion of the boat was too slow for me, and I felt as if I could walk faster, so great was my anxiety to reach my destination. I paced the deck all the time I was on the vessel. It would have been impossible for me to have kept still. But time, no matter how slowly it seems to pass, flies at last, and sooner than I had hoped I found myself approaching the residence of my poor suffering Nita. A young Highland lassie opened the door for me, and when I pronounced my name, led me to a little parlor, with pretty white curtains and neat furniture. The flowers in the vases, which had been carefully arranged by the hand that I knew so well, were withered and faded for want of the tender care they were accustomed to. I did not notice these things at the time, for I could think of but one thing then, and that was my poor Nita, suffering and bereaved, but before I left the house I scanned carefully—oh, how carefully!—everything that had been cherished or tended by her. I was but a few minutes in the room when the door opened and a venerable gentleman entered, who introduced himself as the person who had sent me the dispatch.

"Sir," he said, in answer to the hurried question asked him about my cousin, "she is, we fear, very low. The doctor will be here in a few moments to acquaint you with all the particulars."

As the tears fell from my eyes, this good man seemed touched.

"Dear sir," he continued, "this is indeed a severe trial that God has seemed pleased to afflict you with. We all loved your cousin here as if she were our own. Her husband was my sister's only child, and we were as devoted to his beautiful wife as we were to him."

Here his voice trembled so much that he ceased to

speak. Then I felt how selfish it was in me to think only of my grief when this noble man was so bravely battling against his emotion. I begged him to forgive me for thinking too much of myself, and thanked him for the example of resignation he had set me.

He laid his hand gently on my head as I finished, and said in a kind, tender voice:

"Ah, my son, you are younger by many years than I am, and life's battles seem more difficult to fight in our youth than in mature years, when we think more of the world to come than of this."

Here the doctor entered, and as I went up to him to ascertain his opinion, I saw from the grave expression of his face that he had but little hope for my cousin.

"Sir," he said—in answer to my inquiry, is there no hope?—" in cases of this kind it is better to give explicit answers to relations wishing to know the truth, and I am pained to tell you that there is none. Your young cousin has not many hours for this world."

I shuddered with excessive grief as I walked after the physician, who led the way to Nita's room.

She opened her eyes as I entered and gave a low cry of glad recognition. She raised herself, and in an instant was in my arms. Yes, there at last, after all those years, with no husband between us now. Oh, merciful heaven, for her recovery—to keep her always. But no, God ordained otherwise.

"John, John," she sobbed, "you have come only to see my trouble and sorrow. How differently I expected to meet you! And you did not expect to see me this way when you saw me again, did you, John?"

"Hush, Nita dear. Don't excite yourself. Try to get better, try to, for the sake of the many who are waiting in breathless anxiety to see you well again."

"That they will never see, John—never—never. My heart and my hopes are in my husband's grave, and my body will soon lie by him."

She turned her pale, careworn face from me to the wall as she said this, and the tears chased each other in rapid succession down those thin, white cheeks, which, four years ago, had put the very roses to the blush. The doctor whispered "to say no more, she must be quiet." So when she turned to speak again, I begged her to be quiet and rest.

"It is no use, my dear John, to be so careful of me, for I feel that God will soon give my poor heart a long, long rest. Not many suns will rise for me."

"Oh, Nita," I pleaded, "for the love of heaven do not speak that way. Oh, my dearest, you do not know the wound you are inflicting upon me."

I must have looked my agony, and I think a ray of the real truth dawned upon her then for the first time. I was unable to control this feeling, my grief was so completely mastering me, and my love, which I would have hidden, shown through it and frightened me when I saw that she perceived it. Her pale face grew paler.

"Poor John," she said, "poor, poor cousin! May God bless you ever and ever, my only friend. What would I have done through all these many years if it had not been for you, my brave, noble friend?"

"Do, dear Nita, I beg, say no more."

"I want to speak," she answered, "of a matter of

much importance, and one which lies very near my heart. It is of my poor little baby, so young to lose his mother."

"Yes, Nita," I interrupted her with, "think of that and live."

She answered with a weary smile, and continued:

"John, will you take my poor little orphan and be a father to him. For God's pure love, cherish the little creature. For the sake of his mother, who shared with you all her childish griefs and joys, oh, love my little one, my poor little one."

Her eyelids quivered and the pale lips writhed with pain. I leaned over her and said:

"Nita, I here promise in the presence of God to be a father to your child, to stand by him in adversity and prosperity, to do all that is within me to keep off the rude storms of life from his devoted head, to think first of his soul and body in everything, and my first prayer in the morning and my last at night shall be to call down blessings upon him."

"Then," she said, turning and opening her eyes, in which a peculiar light was shining, "I die happy, and may God listen to the prayer of a dying servant and bless you, my kindest and best friend, forever more."

She lay back with a quiet smile, and I hoped and prayed in my inmost soul that she would return from the dark region of death she had almost reached and live. Towards eve she slept again, but when I lifted her dear head to give the prescribed medicine, she murmured, "No more trouble." I never left her after that. Her night was restless and an uneasy one. The

Highland girl that first met me, and a Sister of Charity, with Sir James, sat up with me. She asked for nothing during that anxious time, though she would often during the night clasp her hands together and repeat her prayers over and over again, and would smile when the Sister, who spent her night on her knees by the bedside, would recite some consoling aspiration. Once she turned, as I smoothed her pillow, and held out her hand, which I took and never relinquished until the angel of death snatched her away from me. She asked for her baby about an hour afterwards. It was brought to her immediately. I held it with one hand, whilst I held her's with the other. She kissed again and again, in passionate tenderness, the little bright face, and I never saw such a look of inexpressible relief and content as when she saw that the little creature took a fancy to me at once, and laid his little face to mine with the winning ways of his mother.

"It will do," she said. "You will love each other."

hen the baby was taken away, I noticed such a change, that I called to the little girl to tell the doctor to come instantly. I was almost beside myself with sorrow. I had hoped until this moment that she would live—until the moment when the doctor entered the room.

"If you have any questions to ask," he said, "now is the time."

I leaned over and said:

"Nita, dearest, have you any message to send to your father or to Eleanor."

"Oh, yes. Tell dear papa that I died blessing him,

and beg him to forgive his poor child and to love for her sake her little Paul; and tell Eleanor I thought of her often in these years of separation, and begged God to aid and bless her in the responsibility she took upon herself. Tell her I trust that her life will be sweet and tranquil, and that we will meet in heaven. And for you, my own dear John, in leaving you my child, I have shown you all my love, my trust, my confidence. Pray God to be merciful to my soul," she then said, as her head sank lower and lower down on the pillow, "and bid my little baby good-bye for his mother. And tell him," she continued, holding my hand and looking into my eyes, "that with my dying breath I resigned him to you, who, after her husband, she loved and esteemed more than any other man on earth."

Here the Sister commenced the prayers for the dying, in which dear Nita joined, and as the last appeal for mercy was uttered, her spirit took its flight to that blessed land where troubles never come and where the weary are at rest.

When the truth flashed upon me, when I fully realized that she had left us forever, when I looked at those beloved eyes and knew that their beautiful light was gone, that those dear lips would speak again no more, and that dear hand would never again hold mine, how hard it was to say "Thy will, not mine, be done!" But at last I said it, and only He whose will it was knows how I was tempted to rebel, and how the solemn promise I made my dying father, to be resigned, was scarce sufficient to overcome the struggle, until my Heavenly Father aided me with His grace.

Oh, surely we are poor and destitute, and without Him can do nothing.

Ah, Nita, Nita, many a long, long, weary year has passed since that sorrowful day when I laid those wasted hands on your quiet breast and consigned you to sleep in the quiet kirkyard, and many a sorrow has pierced my heart, and many a storm of care and trouble passed over my head, silvering it before its time, but none, or all combined, ever thrilled my heart with the deep anguish that sorrowed it on that gloomy day in Scotland, which left me an old man, comfortless, and tired of life whilst still in youth and strength.

CHAPTER XII.

JOHN LOSES HIS BEST FRIEND.

 BROUGHT my little charge home to Ireland, at the urgent request of my cousin, who sent me a message (in answer to the despatch of mine telling the sad news) to that effect. After a last visit to that newly-formed mound, where a coffin made by man's hands could contain so much that was loved and dear, I returned to my home in Erin. I cannot forget how I met an old man with bowed head, whose hairs, age and trouble had left in their winter of life so few and so white, were seemingly uncared for, and fell neglected upon his sorrow-stricken brow. A sadder picture of woe I had never seen, and for the first time I felt there was one who was suffering more than me, caused by that greatest of all griefs, *remorse*. He dropped into my arms as I came up to him. Poor, poor Sir Clarence! My heart bled for the father, and then, for the first time, I forgave him for the pain he had given his younger child.

"You saw her last! you saw her last!" was all he could say, and trembled and sobbed as only an old man can, whose heart is torn by grief, and who knows that time is no more for him in which to rectify his great mistake.

I tried to soothe him as best I could, giving him her last message over and over again as he required, interrupting me every now and then with heart-broken inquiries, and calling upon his lost one to come back once more to her old father.

"Oh, my child! my child!" he would say, "your father did not know when he sent you from him that it would come to this. Oh, God! what have I done? what have I done?"

One day he asked me if she seemed to have suffered much, or ever thought of home or him.

"How could you expect anything else?" I asked, remembering the past with still a bitter pang against this poor old man, who had robbed me of the only pleasure of my life, seeing at times the lost one, and her, who thought of her old home as a kind of Eden, and who, poor and needy as she was, would have gladly given half of her worldly possessions for one more glimpse of the loved place before she was taken to a better land; "her greatest sorrow was your resolute silence," I continued, unable to repress the feeling of resentment I had towards him.

"Oh, darling!" he groaned, in utter agony; "my precious darling! to think that I robbed you of a single happiness! I, that would now gladly lay down my life, and all the other lives that are dear to me on earth, to have you here once more, to have those little arms round my old neck again. Oh, my child! my lost one! and you said you forgave your poor, old, relentless, heart-broken father!"

His grief and remorse seemed to grow every day. Time generally, nay, always, allays sorrow, but in his case it was not so. I noticed his eye, which was once so bright and piercing, grow dimmer, and his light, active step become slower and heavier. He begged me for the little oil painting of her, which I could not refuse the poor old man, though my room looked dark and cheerless when it was taken from it. I never got used to its absence, and used to sigh for it as if it were living. The little Paul was the greatest consolation to me, and he twined himself around my heart with a chain whose links could never be broken. He possessed all the sweet, artless ways of his mother, and kept me continually reminded of some dear trait of hers.

He loved to be with me, and clung to me in sickness and in health. He would appeal to me in his little troubles, and in pain, his little eyes, which were so much like those I had closed, and that were now sleeping, would look at me to soothe him, as if I had the cure in my own hands. He was the most perfect image of baby loveliness and sweetness at night, when his little arms would be wound round my neck, whilst he murmured, in half-broken accents, "God bless me, and make me a dood boy," that I ever saw. Then I would lift my whole soul to heaven, imploring the Divine blessing on this lonely infant head, and beseeching the "Father of the fatherless" to be tender and merciful to this poor little orphan.

To Sir Clarence, too, this little creature was the greatest comfort. Just learning to talk and walk, and with a thousand pretty ways of doing everything and saying everything, each day he became nearer and dearer, and every day brighter and smarter. When he had been with us about three years, there came a great change in poor Sir Clarence. He had never recovered from the dreadful shock the death of the loved one gave him, and which caused him to go to an earlier grave than perhaps he otherwise would have done.

One evening, whilst I was sitting by him in the little study, trying to divert him by reading from an interesting book, I noticed his eyelids droop, for I was very watchful of him in those ways. "Sir Clarence, are you feeling badly?" I asked, as I caught his hand, which felt hot and feverish.

"Yes, my child, I am tired and weary, and wish I could rest."

"Then," I said, "I will help you to your couch, where you can rest whilst I fan you, and perhaps you may fall asleep."

"Thank you, my son, maybe I would feel better; just help me there, and tell me what my poor, lost baby told you when she was dying."

I saw his mind was wandering, and beckoned to one of the servants I saw in the yard to come to me. I sent immediately for the physician, whilst I bathed his forehead and hands in a cooling, healing liquid.

He was restless and uneasy, and would doze away now and then, only to start up to ask something about his children. "Was that Nita's voice I heard singing? Has Eleanor come yet? Where are they? don't let them stay out late, John; little Nita has a cough and these night dews may make it worse." I knew, from many sentences he uttered in his delirium, that he had been thinking a great deal of the few events of our childhood, which I have mentioned, and of Nita's going away. Again he turned to me and said: "Did Sir Charles Stuart take my child from me? and did she go of her own free will? Yes, she went from out that door, and I told her she should never come back again. Eleanor showed great temper in killing the guinea-pig, and poor little baby Nita bore it with such amiability. She is sweeter tempered after all." From other remarks of his, I think he must have been thinking of all the acts of their lives, trying to draw a comparison between them, which was always favorable to Nita. Once he said, whilst I leaned over him bathing his forehead: "John is a good boy, noble, generous and kind-hearted. I can't think he influenced Nita to go with that Scotchman. Oh! if she had only married John, I would so gladly have given my consent, for he is everything I could wish." I heard this last sentence with beating heart and throbbing brain. Then he *had* wished for that union which would have made me supremely happy—but God saw things differently from man, and His holy will be done.

When the physician arrived and had examined his patient, he told me plainly that Sir Clarence's nerves had been so shocked by the blow he had received from his child's death that they could never recover, and that it would only take time to complete the work—and then I knew I must see one more soul that I very tenderly loved take its flight, see one more grave prepared for a dear one, before the same tribute would be paid to me.

"Sir," said the doctor, "I think you had better send immediately for his daughter, for I can promise him but a few days more to live."

I did as he directed, and then sat down by the bedside of this good old man, who had lived a noble, useful life, who had a multitude of friends, and enemies nowhere to be found, and who was fast sinking an unresisting prey to the cruel reaper death, and destined so soon to leave us forever. Little Paul put his head of brown curls into the room, and asked, in a childish whisper, "Mayn't I come to see my grandpapa?" I took him in my arms and held him up to look at his old relative. The little creature must have noticed the great change in him, for he leaned over and touched the aged cheeks with his young lips, and said: "Poor, dear grandpapa is sick!" My cousin opened his eyes and recognized his little grandson.

"My dear little baby! so you have come to see your grandfather before he goes?" and he drew his curly head to him, and kissed the fresh, rosy lips for the last time. He then blessed him and I took him away.

Eleanor came the next day, Sir Clarence, in the meantime, so weak that no one was allowed to enter the room but old Patrick, the doctor and myself. That night, as I was supporting his head, he said to me:

"John, you have been of the greatest comfort to me, my son, and God will bless you. Of course, my child, as his mother, I also leave you unlimited control of little Paul; but John, I would wish that the two little boys, Gerald and Paul, be brought up together, for I wish them to both know and love each other, and form a warm, tender attachment. I will speak to Eleanor, when she comes, upon this matter, and I wish that my dying request should be attended to."

I would have desired this otherwise for many reasons; first, that I did not want Paul to be brought up under Eleanor's roof; and, again, I would rather not live with her myself, which, in this case, I should be compelled to do. Then, again, there were advantages to be derived from this arrangement which I could not help but see. Paul would need a lady with him, as all boys growing up do. If raised with only an old bachelor like myself, he would, I feared, lack the cultivation and refinement which only young men raised by lady-like mothers, or with educated, refined ladies, can acquire, and Eleanor was the only female relative that either of us had that we knew anything about. After her arrival the whole matter was settled. We were to live with her until the children were grown, then the old house in Ireland was to fall to little Paul's share of Sir Clarence's fortune, which was equally divided between his grandsons.

I think Eleanor was really grieved, for the first time since I knew her, when she saw her father's approaching death. I tried to arrange everything exactly as he wished concerning the children, though I saw Paul's aunt was not pleased with the beauty, health and attractive ways of the little orphan, when her own well-attended boy was pale, sickly and irritable. They were kept far away from the sick room, and everything in the house seemed as still and quiet as if it were no longer inhabited.

Two days after Eleanor came we saw the death struggle approaching. I held both of his hands in mine, feeling the pulses grow weaker and weaker.

Eleanor leaned, with her face buried in her hands, near the bed, while the old servants stood around with their sorrowful eyes looking, for the last time, on their old master, who had been a kind, lenient and generous one to them. The doctor was there, too, but his skill was of avail no longer; there was a stronger hand than his at work, and one that had never failed, combat it as you would. I called softly to Eleanor, as I saw that life was rapidly ebbing away. She came and stood by him, but it was my name he called, and I leaned over and heard these last words, "May God and His angels bless——" He could say no more; his eyes closed, that noble heart ceased beating, and the world had lost another good old man.

It was a sad house that we were to leave perhaps forever, and go over to England. I walked around each loved scene, and seemed to love them more and more, as I felt I must leave them for many, many years. Everything was as it used to be when Nita and I played together among the fountains, which were still playing, though we rambled there no more.

Her Nile lilies in the conservatory I went to look at; even they seemed sad, with their heads drooping lowly to the ground. Near the beautiful waters of the Shannon, where I had once heard her sweet, plaintive voice in the evening hymn, I lingered, and thought of how many weary hours I had passed since then, how many a sigh of grief and sorrow had escaped my lips, how many fresh wounds were made in my heart which would never more be healed, and how many more would be there before that loved spot would meet my gaze again. Would the future be quiet and peaceful, or was there still more gloom, more darkness? Was my soul throughout its whole life here to be rent with storms of woe and strife? I shuddered at this thought, for grief makes cowards of us all, and I turned from the anticipation of such a miserable future to the present, to little Paul, of whom I thought most of all, and wondered how, in a strange home and among strange people, he would succeed, and if he would be as happy and joyous as he was now. Here he ran up to me, interrupting my reverie, and I took him in my arms and kissed him, oh, how tenderly!

CHAPTER XIII.

JOHN COMES OVER TO ENGLAND TO LIVE.

WE were over in England at last after many farewells to old servants, who, with tears in their eyes, had bade us adieu, and many longing, lingering looks cast at the old homestead, which stood a fair picture of grandeur, resting on a slight eminence, with its great gables and turrets mounting heavenwards and its shady broad piazzas. Out in the yard, the huge sheltering trees were spreading their great branches, on which were carolling myriads of autumn birds in plaintive melody. My eyes took in at a glance its many charms and attractions as I was slowly leaving the lawn, and everything reminded me of some loved association, or some enjoyment of the past, or brought to mind some fond remembrance of my lost one. After a weary journey of some days, which seemed to fatigue Eleanor and the little boys a great deal, we found ourselves in merry Old England, at our future home—"*Gordon Lodge.*"

To say it was magnificent gives but a partial idea of what it really was. It was a large, beautifully planned mansion, with spacious, pleasant apartments, built with a view to convenience and comfort, and furnished elegantly and tastefully, with all the luxury of a prince. The grounds were laid off after the manner of the Greeks, with many fairy fountains, and sylvan dells carpeted with numerous flowers of every shade and hue, blushing, blooming, and exhaling their delicious fragrance in the air. I felt, whilst gazing on this beautiful picture, as though a magic wand had passed over it, waved by the hand of some fairy queen, for my gaze was fascinated by the beauties it beheld.

In the rear of the building, and some distance from it, in great contrast to the beautiful scene that surrounded me, stood a long and dreary moorland, wide in proportion, and devoid of every vestige of vegetation. At the west end, nearing the sea, I noticed a small grove of dark-looking trees, almost opposite to the Lodge. A peculiar feeling seemed to steal over me as I caught a glimpse of them, they were so different from the trees that I saw in other directions, for the latter were robed in dresses of fresh, bright green, which was cheering to look upon, but here it was dark, dull, and gloomy, and, if I had been of a superstitious nature, I would have thought ominous-looking. That evening, in speaking to Lord Gordon about them, I remarked "that they had a very sombre appearance."

"Yes," he replied, "when I was a boy I was very much afraid of them, they looked so gloomy; but of course I have no such fears now."

"Was their growth spontaneous," I asked, "or were they brought from a foreign soil?"

"They were brought here, of course," he said, laughing, "by the queerest old being that ever laid claim to humanity. An old maiden aunt of my father's, whilst freezing herself away in Norway, happened to spy these uninviting-looking trees, and brought specimens here and transplanted them in their infancy. It seems to me," he went on, "that the whole nature of the trees appear to have changed, perhaps owing to the soil, for I must say that I have never seen trees in the whole course of my life with a more unpromising or doleful aspect."

"They have indeed," was my brief reply, and we dropped the subject, but I felt as if it would have been a relief to have seen them felled.

At first everything in our new home seemed propitious to our comfort and happiness. The beauty and novelty of everything charmed and pleased little Paul, who would often say to me, "Uncle," (for this is what he always called me,) "how beautiful!" or, "Isn't all lovely in aunt Eleanor's house." Eleanor's hard nature seemed to have partially softened after the death of her father, but as months passed away and her grief became less, the harsh tones and cold looks returned. My heart ached each day for my poor little boy, for fear he would not be exempt from them, and well were my fears grounded; for on one summer evening, some five or six months after our arrival, Lord Gordon announced to us that a highly-esteemed friend of his, an old duke from London, would in the course of a few days pay a short visit to the Lodge. Eleanor was too well bred and too well used to society to show any emotion or excitement at the expected arrival, but I noticed that on the particular evening when the duke made his appearance she took great pains in the arrangement of her own toilet and that of her little son, who was, I thought, dressed far too extravagantly, even for a nobleman's child. Little Paul was dressed after my fancy, simply and plainly. When the two little boys came out to me on the piazza, where I sat reading, they certainly presented a very marked contrast—the poor and the rich boy, as they were called. For though Paul would receive one day all my inheritance, which was considerable, he was known only to possess a portion of his grandfather's estate, which was comparatively nothing when compared to the rich lands of Gordon, whose little possessor stood near me arrayed in apparel befitting a young prince. And very much, indeed, did he feel his own importance. But I could not blame the child, for this was altogether his mother's fault. How different from this was the nature of the little boy at my left, whose mind was too noble to harbor either envy or jealousy, and whose soft brown eyes were fixed with a gaze of admiration upon the little lord.

"How much," I said to myself "are these two little ones like their mothers. Perhaps," I thought, as I stroked down the sunny ringlets of the lord's little son, "a nobler nature is enshrined here than is possessed by his fair mother, could but the right hand guide it and lead it aright."

While I thus sat musing, Eleanor came up to us and seated herself beside me on the piazza.

"Don't you think our little lord looks very pretty, John?" she asked, lifting the child to her knee and imprinting a kiss on his delicate cheek. "Why did you not have that child dressed decently?" she continued, without waiting for an answer, and pointing to Paul, "he looks as if he had come out of the ark."

"Never mind Paul," I answered curtly, feeling somewhat hurt that she should have made the remark before the children, "he is pretty enough for all that, let his clothes be what they may."

"It is a good thing," she said, laughing lightly, "that every crow thinks its own the blackest" and gave a fond look at the little boy on her lap.

"I suppose so," was my short answer, as I saw in the distance the carriage of the old duke approaching.

Eleanor made everything unusually attractive and agreeable by being so herself and looking very lovely in her evening costume. She greeted him with peculiar warmth and respect, and I saw that he was both pleased and charmed with the beauty of the woman before him. He was a fine, noble-looking old man, with simple, sweet manners, and possessed the power, which few acquire, of winning one almost at first sight. He was extremely interesting in conversation, and the tones of his voice were soft and pleasant to the ear. He seemed to make himself very much at home at the Lodge, and I found myself each moment growing more and more interested in him.

The evening was passing pleasantly and rapidly away, the sun fast disappearing in the west, as we drew our chairs near the drawing-room window that overlooked the lawn. While we were looking from one bright spot to another, equally admiring each, our eyes fell upon Paul and Gerald playing near a fountain, catching the diamond drops of water ere they fell into the marble basin and then throwing them with merry shouts high into the air.

"Why, my lady," said the duke, addressing Eleanor,

who was seated near him, "you have a little family and have not yet introduced me to it. You were about depriving me of a great pleasure, for I am passionately fond of children."

"I will bring my son here," she said, rising, whilst a smile of pleasure lit up her handsome face. "I wonder that he has not been here long ago to see you. But he seems so interested at present and so busily engaged that he must have forgotten your arrival."

I saw she was delighted that her child had been noticed, and poor thing, when I look back upon it now, I do not wonder, for she had all the love, all the pride of the mother, without the proper judgment or stability to mould the nature of the little being that God had entrusted to her keeping. She brought him in, holding him affectionately by the hand.

As I have said before, he was a pale, delicate child, not unlike his mother in face or disposition, but less irritable and passionate.

The duke took him kindly by the hand and said he was "a real little girl of a boy," and asked why he did not bring his little brother to see him, pointing to Paul, who was still in the yard.

"Oh, that ain't my brother," said Gerald, with something almost amounting to a sneer on his still baby face. "That ain't my brother—that's Paul."

"And pray, who is Paul?" asked the duke, still holding his hand.

"Oh, Paul—why, he's uncle's boy. And ma says that I'm a lord and that Paul is not, and that makes a great difference."

I saw Eleanor's pale face flush scarlet when she heard him tell this truth. She tried to stammer some excuse, but the duke pretended not to have heard the latter part of the boy's speech or to see the mother's confusion. I remained silent, and the duke continued:

"But let me see Paul, too. I love all little boys. I used to have a crowd of my own once, but that was a long, long time ago. They have all grown to great men as large as I am, and I can't call them my little boys any longer."

The child was looking up into the old man's face whilst he was speaking, and there was such a soft look in the old man's eyes as his thoughts went back to those many years ago when his own wee ones were gathered around his knee that the boy was evidently impressed, and said:

"I will call Paul for you if you would like to see him. Shall I go?"

"Yes, my little man," he answered kindly, and the boy left the room and soon returned with his cousin.

"And so, Mr. Meredith, this is your charge," he said, as he placed the child upon his knee and stroked back his soft brown curls, which were clinging to his forehead.

"Yes, he is my charge, and the son of Sir Clarence's youngest daughter, Lady Eleanor's sister."

"Oh, indeed," he replied. "Why, my lady, I never knew before that you had a sister."

"Oh, yes," said Eleanor, who I saw was both disconcerted and angry, but was actress enough to hide her emotion sufficiently to be unperceived by strangers.

"Yes, I had a sister, but the difference in our ages made companionship incompatible. She was married, too, very young, and I never saw her after."

"And this is her only child?" asked the duke, looking at me.

"Yes," I answered, "her only one, and on her death bed he was bequeathed to me."

"I suppose you are very much attached to him."

"Indeed I am," I returned, as I looked at his handsome, honest face and saw all the tenderness and gentleness of his mother in the brilliant brown eyes.

"Yes," said the duke, musing, "he seems to be a very fine child. I almost envy you the possession of him. I would like to raise him myself. There is more character depicted in his little face than is often seen in one so young. And a splendid head, too," he observed, as the little boy came bounding back to tell me his dog had caught a field-lark.

"Come here, Paul, I want to speak to you," he continued, holding out his hand as the child was passing him. "What would you like to make of yourself one of these days?"

"When I am a man, you mean?"

"Yes."

"I don't know," said the boy. "My uncle says I must not want to hold any office or be anything that is not for my country's good, and that I must try to be an honor to my country. So I suppose that I will be a soldier, and then I can fight for her."

"Well said, my little hero," the old man replied. "A brave man always honors his country by fighting for it."

Paul then left us, and we all sat for a moment in silence in the coming twilight. I felt rather sorry for Eleanor when all these compliments were lavished upon Nita's child and her own passed by unnoticed. I thought, too, that it was an unhappy event for Paul, for I knew she was jealous of him, and the poor child would have more to suffer because of his lovely ways and handsome face.

The duke spent some time with us, and seemed pleased with the freshness of the country scene, whilst the pure air of the healthy locality lent vigor and strength to his frame. Lord Gordon seemed very fond of this old friend of his, and never tired of entertaining him or pointing out to him the beauties of his estate. One day I was particularly struck that he noticed, as I had when I first came to the Lodge, the grove of dark firs, and said to Lord Gordon:

"Truly, my lord, that is an unsightly-looking clump of trees. I think if I were a highwayman I would take my stand there and feel no apprehension of being discovered."

Lord Gordon said:

"Yes, people generally noticed the gloom of the place, which was deepened by a superstition attached to it."

"What is it?" we both asked, eagerly.

"Why, it is said, that when my old grandaunt, who was crazy with eccentricity, planted them there, she prophesied, 'that as long as they stood and flourished the Gordons would prosper; but when they fell, woe to the House of Gordon, for that also would fall.'"

"That's strange," we both said, musing.

"Oh, no!" he answered, laughing; "eccentric people possess a fund of imagination from which they generally create dark and gloomy pictures."

"That's true," was the quiet answer of the Duke's, and we dropped this subject which had been renewed for the second time.

The next day the old man left us. He had given us much pleasure by his presence, and with many regrets we bade him adieu. And now to return again to Eleanor and to the boys. The old Eleanor Graham was returning day by day; the cold, unkind manner, the haughty, imperious temper, the harsh and severe tones—and I felt more for little Paul in those days than I did even in years after, for she tyrannized over him when I was not by, and the little life that should have been all sunshine was made sad and unhappy.

I noticed one night, when the children were in bed, and their brown and fair curls pillowed on their downy cushions, that Eleanor came to tell her son good night, which she always did, and passed by the couch of Paul without noticing him. I had often, in nights before, when I went to bid him good-night, noticed the tear drops on his glowing cheek, and I ventured to ask:

"What is the matter, my boy?"

"Why is it, uncle," he asked, "that aunt Eleanor never bids me good-night? I am sure I would be very happy if she would. You always kiss Gerald good-night, and why can't she kiss me?"

"Never mind, my darling," I said; "she does not

intend to be unkind, it is only forgetfulness." So, when I saw the silken lashes resting upon each cheek, and heard the drowsy voice say "good-night," I stole softly to Eleanor's chamber. She was sitting near the open window, and I seated myself in the vacant chair beside her.

"Eleanor," I began, "why is it that you cannot be more affectionate in your manner to poor little Paul? I am sure you could at least give him a good-night kiss, and the little creature's heart would be so much lightened by it; he, child as he is, notices how very different your manner is to him than to Gerald."

"And, indeed, sir," she said, with fire flashing in her eyes, "I want everybody to notice the difference. Do you think," she continued, "that I, too, am going crazy over that child, who is already as full of conceit as if he were a man of twenty-five? I think, for my part, that you are crazed on this subject. You are making yourself ridiculous about him. Yes, I do want everybody to see that my child is preferred to him, and everybody to know it."

"But, Eleanor," I said, "just for once put by prejudice, and look with a just eye upon the matter. Would it either injure you or your child to be kind and just to a little orphan—one whose mother was your sister—and is it right in you to nourish the idea of this false pride and vanity in your son that he is superior to Paul and to other children? No, Eleanor Gordon; the day may yet come when you will wish that you had listened to advice, and treated with more care and tenderness the little boy whose mother is sleeping under the sod,"

"You are very good at giving lectures, Mr. Meredith, I see," she said, haughtily, "but I beg that in future you will confine them to those who may need them and will be profited by them; as for myself, I feel that I am a responsible being, and quite capable of managing my own affairs without the aid of others."

"You are not so perfect, Eleanor," I answered, "that a little advice now and then would not help you if you would receive it properly."

"Then, when I want it," she said, "if you are the proper person, I will ask you for it."

I could say no more to this woman, who, like many more in this world, imagined herself infallible. She would not be reasoned with, and her love for her child was such that she would uphold him in right or wrong. I heard a good man say once that this was not love but rather an infatuation, this blindness to the imperfections of their children—that true love sought out their faults and corrected them—and I feel that he was right.

My business in London caused me several trips during the year. I always left little Paul behind me at Gordon Lodge, because my time would be so employed that I could not pay him the necessary attention. On returning from one of these visits, I found the little boy looking weary and sad, with bright, feverish spots on his cheeks, and noticed that he clung closer and closer to me all the day, rather after the manner of a little girl than little boy. I put my arm around him, and asked what was the matter, and why did my boy look so sad; that was not the way for a little man to do, he ought to run, and play, and be merry.

"Oh! I don't want to, uncle," he said, and the tears came welling into his eyes. "I feel sick, too, and Gerald says that my mamma ran away and got married and broke poor grandpapa's heart, was disobedient and didn't do right at all. I got mad, and said it was not so, and Gerald said it was, and that I was nothing but a pauper, for aunt Eleanor said so, and that my mother was no better; and then I knocked him down, uncle, for I couldn't help it. I'll not have such things said of my mamma, who, you have told me, was so good and lovely. And then Gerald cried, and aunt Eleanor said I was a bad, naughty boy and locked me up in the cellar."

I, too, told him he was a naughty boy for knocking his cousin down, who was much smaller than he was; but seeing he was sick, I gave him a cooling draught, and soon saw him sink into a restless, feverish slumber, and I went to enquire the particulars. I met old Patrick, who was still with us, on the staircase. I called him into my room and bade him to tell me the whole circumstance of Paul's disgrace, if he knew anything about it.

"I say this, young Masther" (for thus he still called me), "it is a downright shame the way in which Lady Eleanor treats that child. I can hardly stand it, sometimes, when I think about it."

"But how did it all happen?" I asked.

"Well, they were playing in the hall," commenced the old man, "and when I heard their voices take a very high pitch, I stepped up on the piazza to know what it was all about. I heard Gerald speaking to

Paul about his mother in a very bad manner, and Paul's face grew redder and redder, until at last he did just what I would have done, young Masther—he knocked Gerald down, and the spoilt youngsther howled at such a rate that his mother came running to know what was the matther."

"Are you sure," I asked, "that Paul was not in the wrong?"

"No, indeed!" he answered; "I am only sorry that he didn't hurt that little Vandal when he knocked him down."

"Don't say that, Patrick," I said, "for you are as much prejudiced in Paul's favor as Eleanor is in Gerald's."

"I am prejudiced on the side of justice," he said, with emphasis.

"Well, well, then; what next?" I asked, knowing it was useless to continue in this strain with the old man.

"Well, she gave him a blow on the cheek, and 'tis true her hand is tiny and fair, but he felt it as much as if it had been dealt by a larger, rougher hand, and, I believe in his heart felt it worse, and then she locked him up in the cold, damp cellar, and kept him there for five long hours. I went to her often and often during the day to beg the release of her little prisoner, but this she would not grant me, and refused to see me at last when I came so often; but when evening came on, Lord Gordon interfered, and said the child must be released; and when I brought him from his gloomy cell he was stiff and cold. All the servants said it was a shame, and I was not afraid to tell my Lady so, and that I would tell my young Masther when he came back. She gave me the look Eleanor Graham used to give me of old, but I cared little for that."

Patrick was a true Irishman, full of justice and bravery—the characteristics of the whole nation—and at length he left me, after taking a look at the little sleeper who was dozing away on the lounge, still in a kind of stupor, from which I did not know whether to rouse him or not. I leaned over and kissed his warm cheek, and then went to look for Eleanor.

CHAPTER XIV.

PAUL'S SICKNESS.

 FOUND her in the garden, whiling away the time, attending her flowers, and giving directions concerning them.

"Well, John, so you've come back; how are you?" and she greeted me in the usual manner.

"Yes, I have gotten back, and am quite well, I thank you, and hope that you are, too."

"Oh, yes!" she answered, gaily, "but just come here and look at my spring roses. I think they are perfect beauties. Andrew, the gardener, says they are the prettiest in the country, though Lady Lilian Grantly thinks hers surpass anything in Christendom. I am very sure, though, that she hasn't seen mine; just look here, have you ever seen anything half so lovely?" as we nea•l the bushes of brilliant, fragrant roses mingled together in rich profusion.

"Yes," I said, "they are a rare treasure, truly," and we walked on for a few moments in silence, which I at length broke, by saying:

"Eleanor, since I came I have heard of the quarrel between Paul and Gerald. I do think it was very naughty in Paul to have knocked his little cousin down, but he had just provocation, I have no doubt, and Eleanor, do you think it was just to have punished him as severely as you have done?" I spoke very calmly, but it required a great effort to control myself when I thought of the cruel injustice practised upon the little boy who had no mother and none but me to plead his cause.

"Do you think it severe treatment?" she said; "indeed, I do not. Had it not been for Lord Gordon it would have been doubly as severe, for he richly deserved it."

I could scarcely believe that a woman so beautiful could be so inhuman and for a moment I was mute; at length I said:

"I am glad to see, Eleanor, that your husband is just, and, hereafter, when Paul Stuart needs chastisement, I will administer it to the exclusion of everyone else." How gladly I would have taken the little boy in my arms and carried him forever away from the influence of this woman, had it not been for the dying request of Sir Clarence; and, oh! how often and often I tried to make these two little boys love each other as he wished, but it seemed all in vain. There was something about Gerald that excited my compassion; it was true he was a martyr to his pride and very selfish, but then he was such a fragile, delicate little creature that I could not have been unjust to him even if I had tried, and it would have done my heart good could I have seen these two grow up with the affection of brothers as their poor old grandfather wished.

I walked back to my chamber to see how the child I had left there was faring, for he was to me as the tender ivy clinging to the strong wall. I found him delirious and feverish, and my worst fears realized. The poor boy had a raging fever, which made me almost wild with anxiety. When the physician came, he told me that his young life hung upon a thread. I felt a suffocating feeling rise in my throat. What could I do without this young child, that had his mother's face, his mother's eyes, her thousand winning ways, and all her nobleness of disposition. He was all on earth I cared for then—at least it seemed so to me—all the rest appeared as a shadow to the sun in comparison to this boy. Day and night I watched every movement of his head, heard each cry of pain, attended to every want, and found my devotion growing deeper and deeper.

Old Patrick, too, appeared never to weary at the sick couch, seeming to rival me in his attentions. And, indeed, it was true that this little sick boy held the chords of his heart as well as mine. The physician was a kind, good man, who seemed most anxious about his patient, and never before had I felt that any human being gave me the same amount of comfort in the same length of time. One day he said to me, whilst we were sitting by the bedside of the sufferer:

"Mr. Meredith, I cannot tell how this little child of yours has interested me. He is almost as dear to me as if he were mine. He is truly the most manly little boy I ever saw, and is very prepossessing."

I gave him my hand, for my heart was too full for me to speak, and in that grasp we vowed eternal friendship; and together we saw the little fellow grow strong, until at last he was convalescent.

CHAPTER XV.

PAUL BECOMES A HERO.

NEVER left little Paul alone again at the Lodge after he recovered from his illness. He was growing in strength and manliness, and my heart was becoming more and more attached to him every day. During the spring days which were bright and cheering, I used to take the little boys every evening for a walk. In these rambles I would relate to them anecdotes instructive and amusing, which they seemed to relish with a great deal of gusto. On one of these evenings we had walked a considerable distance to a part of the country which was not as open as that in which we lived, and where hills were studded here and there, and between them situated pleasant but narrow valleys, through which murmured many a crystal brook over its pebbly bed. We stood on a slight eminence, gazing with admiration on the many country seats scattered around, which were undergoing summer repairs for their owners, who were still enjoying London life. While we were thus gazing and pointing from one lovely scene to another, Paul called my attention to a little white cottage nestled among some aged trees, whose huge branches seemed to shelter it with their dense foliage. It was a pretty little cot, so snowy white, and with its ivy vines climbing up the lattice on the back piazza, while in front luxuriant honey-suckles twined with the wild rose in beautiful disorder. The yard was rather large

for the little white house that stood within it, but still it was all so neatly laid off in pretty flower-beds that you scarcely noticed the great difference. There was a gentle slope in the yard to the left, which ended in a small natural lake, whose waters were smooth and clear, and on whose border grew many a pale water-lily. It was altogether a charming little spot, and I was not surprised when I saw Paul clap his hands and exclaim:

"Oh, what a pretty place! I would like to live there myself."

"Do you know who lives there, uncle?" asked Gerald.

"No," I said, "but we can go to that tree yonder and get a nearer view of it."

So we walked a few yards further down to a neighboring beech and stood beneath its shade whilst we continued to look upon the little cottage. In one of its windows hung a cage with a little canary, which was warbling away its sweetest music and seeming to enjoy above all things the soft spring sunshine. A little girl came to the window and threw in a handful of seed to the bird, who picked them up in his bill, apparently with the greatest relish. Then the little girl came forth from a side door, holding a white kitten locked in her arms, and with two tiny white bare feet traveled with rapidity down to the lake. As she came towards the water, she approached much nearer to us, and I had a full view of the little figure, which was clothed in a blue gingham dress, with a low-necked, short-sleeved white apron. There was something unusually winning and interesting about her, and as Paul whispered, "Oh, uncle, how pretty!" I bowed my head, for there was something about this fair young child that instinctively attracted me towards her.

"There, she wants to get into that boat, uncle," said Paul, "and if she does she may fall into the water. May I go down to her?"

"No," I answered, "wait a few moments and let us see what she will do."

So we stood, unperceived by the child, who was making vigorous attempts to reach the boat, but all in vain.

"Now, kitty," she said, addressing the cat, who looked up and mewed, as if it understood every word she uttered, "will you run away if I put you down? If you do, you will be a naughty kitten, and I won't love you a bit."

She held up her finger to the cat, as if to make her words more impressive. The act was so gracefully and artlessly done, that I very naturally exclaimed:

"What a beautiful little creature!"

She put the kitten down, and it seemed so fully to appreciate its freedom, that, with a shake of its body and another mew, which I suppose was meant for a farewell, it bounded off at full speed.

"Oh, kitty, kitty," she cried, "you are a naughty kitty. Come back to me."

But the kitty heeded not the cry and fled on, with the little girl after it. Paul was all eagerness to assist her in her chase, while Gerald wanted to kill the cat; but I checked them till I heard the child give a cry of pain when she saw her kitty clinging to the stalk of a water-lily upon the very edge of the lake.

I could detain Paul no longer. He sprang like a young Highlander from point to point on the hill till he had reached the foot of it, and then ran at full speed to the edge of the pond, where he rescued the cat, and laid it safely in its mistress' arms. She looked up into the boy's face, with a glance of admiration from the most expressive grey eyes I ever looked at, and then exclaimed:

"Why, where did you come from? I didn't see you here anywhere?"

"Oh, I saw you on the hill there," said Paul, "trying to catch your kitten, and I came down and caught it for you. But I wanted to speak to you anyhow," he said, in his honest, frank way.

"And I think you a nice boy, and I like you. Now tell me what your name is and I will tell you mine."

"Paul," he answered.

"And mine is Amy."

"Amy what?" I asked, as I came up and broke in upon this childish conversation.

"Amy Wayland," she answered.

"And do you live there?" I asked, pointing to the white house.

"Yes, I live there with my papa and my mamma."

"And have you no brothers or sisters?"

"No, sir, there is nobody but me. I had a little sister last spring, but they took her away, and mamma says she is sleeping yonder," nodding her head in the direction of a little graveyard resting on the side of the hill.

"Do you know who made you, little one?" I asked, patting her on her head.

"Yes," she said, "God."

She then took her kitten and poked its nose up into Gerald's face, saying:

"Kiss my kitten. I kiss it often."

"I won't kiss your ugly kitten," he said, furiously. "I won't kiss it, and I don't think it's nice in you to kiss it either."

She turned away very much disconcerted, and walked up to Paul, saying:

"I don't like him. You wouldn't mind kissing my kitten, would you?"

"I would rather kiss you," he answered.

"Would you?" she said, with a pleased look. "That's what mamma says when I ask her to kiss my kittie."

"She has good taste," I chimed in, and leaned over and kissed the cherry lips myself, and as the sun was sinking rapidly in the west, we bade the little girl adieu and turned our faces homeward.

"Uncle," said Paul, "that was a sweet little girl, wasn't she? and I liked to talk to her."

"I don't think she was nice a bit," said Gerald, "putting her old kitten up into my face and telling me to kiss it. And she wasn't dressed nice either. I can't like her not having on nice clothes."

"My child," I said, "God often loves those dearest whom he clothes in the poorest raiment. Never judge of people by their clothes, or draw your likes or dislikes from them."

The boys said no more, and I thought, as I had often thought before, had Gerald been away from his mother's influence and example, he would have been a different being.

Very often after that we saw little Amy Wayland, who sometimes came to the Lodge with an old nurse to bring Paul flowers that grew on her favorite bushes. The children played together, and seemed to enjoy amazingly having a little girl with them. I used to sit on the piazza (for I always loved children) and watch the three in the yard at play, wondering if in after years these three little life paths would converge or diverge. Noticing all the while the three characters that must one day be formed either for good or for evil, I could not help seeing how manly and gentle little Paul was to the young girl he christened "Fairy." She would cling to him for protection, while she and Gerald were always at open warfare—I must say that Gerald was always the attacking party—while Paul would coax until he would get them into a good humor without using any violence on either side.

Although there were but three months difference in these boys ages, still there were years in other respects, and Paul seemed to have the advantage.

Eleanor even noticed the exceeding beauty of Amy, and told me "she thought it would be dangerous for the boys if she continued to grow as pretty, for all boys go crazy over a pretty face, and either of them may forfeit his position in order to marry her."

I laughed, for what she said seemed ridiculous, and answered, "that if Paul chose to fall in love with her when he was grown he could do so with my full permission and consent."

"And you don't know even who she is?" said Eleanor, with some warmth.

"I know," I answered, "that she is a very sweet child, and I am sure her mother is a lady."

"That is not sufficient for me," she exclaimed, turning away, "and when she grows larger she must be kept away from my house altogether."

I smiled to myself as she made this remark, as I thought it very silly; for I did not know how it would all be in years to come.

One evening I missed the three children from the yard, where they had been playing. I had been reading, and was so deeply interested in my book that when I finished I missed them for the first time, and could find them nowhere. It was very heedless in their attendants not to have been with them, but Eleanor and Lord Gordon were in London, and in their absence the servants at the Lodge seemed to desire a holiday, and I could hardly blame them, for they had a right hard time of it other days. I went to look for the two boys who usually attended Paul and Gerald, but one of them, I was told, was bird hunting, and the other had gone some distance in the country to see his grandmother. I was very much provoked when I heard this piece of news, and continued myself the search for the missing ones. I walked through the great avenue of trees, through the park, where deer were feeding leisurely here and there, but I could not find them. I was very uneasy when I went to the summer houses in quest of them and found them vacant. I called aloud, but no voice answered me, and indeed my heart beat fast when no servant could give me any information about the chilnren. At last, I called Patrick to assist me in the hunt. We searched high and low, and called and called, but nowhere did I hear a voice or the sound of a footstep. I don't know what made me think of the several small isles in the sea, where we often used to row for pleasure in the evenings, but to them I directed my steps with all haste. As I neared the shore, where the small vessel was anchored that used to convey persons over to the isles, I found it missing. I called the names of the children aloud, when Gerald's voice answered me, and looking across the nearest little patch of terra firma, I saw them, and at a glance took in their positions. Gerald was standing on a very safe place—he always managed to take care of number one; I did not blame the boy for this self-preservation, for we all know it is the first law of nature—but my heart seemed to stop beating when I saw the other two children. The little girl had fallen into the water, and even her glossy curls were hidden beneath the waves; one small arm was lifted up, with its tiny hand clasping Paul's, who was standing with one foot in water and one on land, with one hand catching a bending seaweed and the other holding firm and fast the little girl. I was an expert swimmer; so throwing off my coat, I was soon out on the briny deep, going with all haste to the rescue of the two children.

I was just in time, for as I caught those two little clasped hands in my broad palm the sea-weed broke,

and if it had not been for my timely aid these little
ones would have gone to a watery grave. Amy was
unconscious, whilst Paul's young limbs were strained
and ached from being kept in one position so long.
Fortunately for us the boat was but a few yards distant; we were soon in possession of it and sailing back
to the shore, which I had no sooner reached, than I
ran with all possible haste, the little unconscious burden in my arms, to my old friend, the doctor, who had
saved Paul in his dangerous illness, and who, when he
saw me, came in haste to know what was the matter.
He took the child from me into his stout arms as if she
had been a baby, and carried her to his house, where
we were met by his wife, who was kind and ladylike,
rendering us every assistance. The old kind-hearted
doctor insisted upon my changing my apparel for some
of his own until I could do better. Then he turned
his attention to the child, who lay with her eyes closed
and every particle of life seemingly extinct.

I felt very miserable sitting there holding those small
hands, feeling the pulses throbbing slowly and faintly,
and, as I thought, forever away; and picturing to myself the agony of the poor mother when she heard the
terrible news. I thought of sending for her, thinking
the child in a much more dangerous condition than she
really was; and when I spoke of it to the doctor, he
said, in his good-humored way, "not to be crazy, and
kill the mother before the child was dead." Seeing the
philosophy of the remark, I sat down again, and soon
had the happiness of seeing life take a strong hold, and
then possession altogether, under the medical treatment

of Dr. Arnold. I had sent home for the pony-chaise to take the little girl home, and when it arrived she was ready to go with me. She sat in my lap as I drove the pony along through the beautiful country, telling me all the circumstances of the adventure. They had all gone to the small island to get some flowers that grew upon it, and "I being too near the edge, fell in, and if it hadn't been for Paul, would have been drowned."

"Didn't you know it was very naughty to have gone there at all, you three little ones, by yourselves?" I asked.

"Yes," she said, "it must have been very naughty, but we never thought of that, and please don't tell my papa;" and there was a frightened look upon her face which I never saw there before. "I am sure my mamma will be so glad to know that I am saved, but papa will be very angry if he hears that I had gone there."

I promised that I would not, and we soon reached the cottage, nestling among the trees, looking so cool and pleasant. The door was opened to us by the old woman who used to bring Amy to the Lodge.

"Is my papa at home, Nellie?" enquired the child.

"No, deary," she replied, and she took the child in her arms, as if she understood why the question was asked.

I asked to see Mrs. Wayland, for I thought it was only right that she should be made acquainted with the adventure. I was taken into a little parlor, and was at once struck with the refined look of everything. 'Tis true the furniture was old-fashioned, but it was highly polished, and there was an air of taste in the arrangement of it. On the tables and brackets there were vases of flowers, filled with the freshest and fairest of spring's floral gifts, filling the whole room with fragrance.

I was seated opposite the mantel, and over it I noticed the portrait of a young girl who was very fair and lovely, and there was something about the calm, sweet expression that reminded me of a face I had seen in years gone by and which was still impressed upon my heart, though I had only seen it with boyish eyes and loved it with boyish heart: it was the face of my own fair mother. I had pushed open one of the shutters to gaze at it more fully, when the door opened and a lady entered. Amy said "Mamma," and I rose and introduced myself. I felt very much interested in her as she approached and held out her hand with such a look of gratitude in her face. I at once recognized the likeness to the picture, but a change was there which was surely not caused by years, for she was still a young woman. The face now wore a very sad expression, which moved me, and I would have given a great deal to have known something of her past history. I related the occurrence of the evening, and noticed how she pressed the form of her only child to her heart, smothering the beautiful face with warm and tender kisses. Once the little girl asked something about her papa. 'Twas then I saw a look of mingled fear and contempt pass over the lady's face, which she in vain strove to conceal; but it was very apparent to me. I left her after a few more remarks of civility, much pleased with what I saw and deeply interested in Mrs. Wayland, in whom I recognized, in every sense of the word, a lady. She had begged me to call often, telling me that I little knew all I had done for her in saving the life of her little one. I promised to come often and bring Paul, who had turned out a hero at the age of eleven.

CHAPTER XVI.

JOHN DISCOVERS SOME RELATIONS.

THE small town of L—— lay some ten miles to the west of Gordon Lodge. It was well built, pleasantly situated, and healthfully located, with many handsomely-built dwellings and wealthy factories. I had for convenience concentrated all of my business here, and one evening, weary and tired, as I was returning from this town, after a day of many business transactions that were both tedious and disagreeable, I was riding along the edge of the moorland on horseback, for I was still fond of this mode of traveling. As I approached the grove of dark firs I saw a man leaning against one of them in a hunting-jacket, with his arm resting carelessly on his gun. He was a slight, handsome man, and his attitude was fearless and manly. I could not tell what it was that made me shudder, but think it must have been the man's position. He seemed to be of a most companionable disposition, for as I advanced towards him he mounted his horse and joined me with a bow graceful enough for a cavalier in the time of chivalry. We were soon chatting very pleasantly together, and I would have thought him on the whole a very estimable companion but for a restless, unquiet look in the eye which I did not like to encounter. In the course of our conversation he told me his name, which was Godfrey Laughton, and the owner of a very beautiful country seat about three miles from the

Lodge, known as "Merry Hall," for this young man was much given to pleasure and sport, and thus appropriately named his place. His origin was completely unknown, though when he first came into the country he was supposed to be a Pole from his foreign appearance, but soon became anglicized in custom and manner, though few cared to know where he came from. He was wealthy and dashing, driving the finest horses, giving the most fashionable dinners, and furnishing the best of wines most lavishly, which made him very popular amongst the young men, while mammas with marriageable daughters looked at the handsome Hall and then at the handsome man, and between the two he was completely lionized.

Our conversation naturally turned on the people of the country as we passed some of their country seats, and he told me there were a great many families coming down that season who were in the habit of going to German watering places.

Just here we came upon little Amy Wayland and her old nurse, who were taking an evening promenade. I stooped down and shook the small hands that were held up to me, whilst Godfrey Laughton ran his hands through her silken curls, saying:

"How is my little girl this evening?"

"I'm well," was the short and, I thought, curt answer, as she turned away from him and spoke to me, and during the rest of our conversation she merely answered him in monosyllables, without looking at him.

I could not help noticing this, thinking it was rather strange, and wondering what was the dislike the child could have for him. After we had left and ridden some distance he turned to me and said:

"You have seen that child before, I see."

"Oh, yes," I said, "I have seen her several times."

"She is a very beautiful thing," was his rejoinder, "and has a very sweet mother."

"Yes, I have seen her, too," was my reply.

"Have you, indeed," he said, significantly, "then I suppose you have seen her husband also?"

"No; I have never met him. I suppose you have had that honor, though."

"Oh, yes; we have been friends ever since we met in her Majesty's service some three years ago. He was captain of a company in a foot brigade, and I belonged to the same regiment."

"Then you are an Englishman," I said; "but you seem to me to look rather young to have belonged to a regiment some three years ago."

I thought there was a slight hesitation in his voice as he answered:

"Yes, but I was always older than my looks, and I joined the regiment anyhow."

I was but half satisfied when I heard him say this, and rode on for a few moments without speaking. Then to break this silence, which was embarrassing, I remarked:

"So you know the Waylands?"

"Oh, yes."

"Are they from this part of the country?" I asked.

"No, no," he said; "the captain met Mrs. Wayland in Ireland. She was spending some time at her uncle's, who lived on the banks of the Lee. He was wounded in a duel fought with a fellow-officer, and was taken to the house of Miss Oswald's uncle by the request of a friend, who obtained permission for him to be carried there "——

"Miss who?" I interrupted, as the name seemed to strike a chord in my memory.

"Miss Oswald," he repeated.

I remembered then the reason the name was familiar. My mother had a sister who married a Captain Oswald, and I have often heard her spoken of when a child by my father and mother. I remained silent, and Laughton went on:

"Then it was the old story over again—the fair lady fell in love with the wounded soldier. But the girl's uncle refused his consent to her marriage, for he had taken some dislike to the captain, and then they, as most couples do under the same circumstances, had recourse to an elopement. I don't know much about Captain Wayland myself," he continued, "but think that he is a very good fellow and quite a jovial companion. People will say that elopements turn out very unhappily, but for my part I think this case an exception."

I was not of his opinion, when I remembered the sorrowful looking face and the sad eyes of poor Mrs. Wayland, which had so impressed me.

After I had parted with Godfrey Laughton, and on my way home, I was putting, as the old saying is, two and two together, and wondering if this gentle lady could be any relation of mine; the resemblance in the portrait to my dead mother was truly very striking, and this name of Oswald, which I had heard so often when a boy, and which had been so familiar, seemed strange. How very singular it would all be if she were a relative, I kept thinking, and what a double interest I would take in little Amy. The subject engrossed me nearly all evening, and before dismissing it, I determined to go the next day to see Mrs. Wayland and ascertain if she would not say something to me of her past history. I trusted, though, that the discovery would be as I wished, for I was already very fond of these two, the mother and the child. The next morning, immediately after breakfast, I peeped into the window of the school room and nodded at the two boys, bidding them be good whilst I was away. Paul's bright eyes glistened, and he seemed so anxious to go with me that it pained me to refuse, but I had my set rules and would not break in upon the school hours. I started, unable to control my anxiety any longer, to find out as much as I could of the history of Mrs. Wayland. It was a lovely spring morning, and the birds were warbling their rich notes upon every hedge and bough, the daisies and buttercups were sprinkled over the grass, gently waving their heads before the soft spring zephyr. This was a trying time to me, and perhaps if nature had not been so consoling with her smiling face, my heart might have been very heavy, for I hardly knew what the disclosure I was in search of would bring forth. My relations were the only persons with whom I was intimate, and all my sorrows had arisen in my own family out of it; I had scarcely known care, for my acquaintances were few. As I neared the cottage I saw little Amy run from the house, slamming the door behind her. I naturally hurried on to bid her good morning, and as I opened the little wicket gate was somewhat surprised to see the child crouching beneath one of the rose bushes, evidently anxious to hide herself. I walked forward, and what was my surprise to see tear drops on her rosy cheeks. I picked her up in my arms and asked her what was the matter. She only answered me with a low sob, as she nestled her head upon my shoulder. I carried her to the house, still in my arms, and noticed that she trembled at every step. I reached the porch and was just about to lay my hand upon the door, when it was opened from the inside, and I met, face to face for the first time, Captain Wayland. A more repulsive-looking man could scarcely be imagined; his face was bloated with dissipation and wore a scowl that was truly forbidding. The child clutched me tighter the instant he made his appearance.

"So, my little Miss," he broke the silence, without noticing me, "you ran away from me, did you? but you shall be paid for all this."

He attempted to snatch her from my arms, but I waved him back.

"Who are you?" he said, with an angry frown. "Who dares interfere between me and my child?"

"When you are cool, Captain Wayland," I answered, "I will cease to interfere; but whilst you are in this passion you shall not touch this poor little one."

He tried again to snatch her from me, but she clung

to me, entreating that I would not let her papa take her.

As the child pronounced my name in her entreaties, a complete metamorphosis took place in the man's face. I would scarcely have recognized it as the same scowling, repulsive face that met me at the door. He turned to me with a smile and a bow, and with the most gentlemanly and hospitable manner invited me to enter. Why this change should have taken place I never understood, unless he knew me to be connected with the powerful house of Gordon, or had heard of my wealth, for I believe I was reputed to be a very rich man. I returned his courtesy by entering and enquiring for Mrs. Wayland.

As I noticed his bland, captivating manners, which I knew to be assumed, I was not surprised that the poor wife was so easily duped. She at last entered, and as I addressed my entire conversation to her, Captain Wayland shortly after arose, made his excuses and withdrew. There was a tired look on her face, and I saw, too, that her eyes were as much swollen as her child's. She was sitting on the end of a small sofa, with her elbow resting on its arm, and her hand supporting her fair head. There was something that attracted me very much to this Mrs. Wayland, something that I could not define; perhaps it was because she was so young and seemed to have suffered so much. Her face, though so fair, was furrowed by many a line of grief and care, and that white brow, on which the brown hair was modestly and plainly parted, through which a silver strand could be seen here and there, to my eye was very sad, for I am sure the lady could not have exceeded more than nine-and-twenty, but, like many a young life, it was wrecked in its springtime. Our conversation was quiet and pleasant, for with me she seemed to be very much at ease, and she had an easy, modest way about her which invited one's confidence, and which to me was very pleasing. On a table near me, on which my arm was resting, I noticed a worn volume of "Thomas A 'Kempis," which seemed to have been much used. It was opened with its face downwards. I raised it as it lay, and saw that it was open at the chapter, "Son, I am the Lord who gives strength in the day of tribulation." I ran my fingers through the book, and found, on the fly leaf, in a woman's delicate handwriting:

"To my little daughter, Geraldine, on her 6th birthday.
"Sept. 5th; Oak Grove, on the James,
"Virginia."

"That is my little book, and it is the source of great consolation to me," she said, as she watched me looking through it.

"Yes," I answered, "and it is a very precious little volume; but is this your name written here?"

"Yes," she replied.

"And is this your birth-place, on the banks of the James?"

She nodded in the affirmative.

"Then you are a Virginian," I said, astonished, "and living away over here from your beautiful land?"

"Yes," she said, "it is indeed a lovely country; but after the death of my mother, who was an Englishwoman, I was sent to my relations in Ireland, my father's brother, where I was raised on the banks of the Lee instead of the James. My father was a captain in the United States Navy, and died in the service of that country whilst I was still very young."

I could scarcely control my impatience to know her mother's name until she had finished speaking, and then I quickly asked:

"Mrs. Wayland, what was your mother's name?"

"Mary Eastern," she replied, somewhat surprised at the abrupt manner in which I put the question.

"Had she a sister?" I asked.

"Yes, only one, who was some years younger than herself. There were only the two children, who were unfortunate enough to have lost their mother whilst both were very young."

"What was her name?" I said, almost breathless, for so much depended upon her answer.

"Angela; and I have so often heard my mother speak of her beautiful young sister."

Here I interrupted her, saying,

"Mrs. Wayland, do you know that you are my cousin?" and took her hand.

"What?" she said, with a new light in her eyes, and her face becoming perfectly beautiful; "what! you my cousin? my aunt Angela's child whom my mother so fondly loved, and who I was taught always to love and pray for? You her child? then God has indeed blessed me, for I am sure you will pity me and not forsake me as my other relations have done."

Here the old, sad look returned, and I felt that I could almost weep for her.

"Forsake you? No! never, Geraldine; and God has blessed me, too, in giving me you for a friend, so gentle and loveable."

We sat a long time together, and she told me of her past history; how she had suffered and how she had forfeited the love of that noble uncle who had taken her to his heart, and who had been a kind father to her, loving her as one of his own offspring; but now, through her own fault, she was an exile, away from her home, where she had been a pride and a darling. "But I suppose I deserve it all," she said, with a sigh of resignation; "and if God will spare me to be a protector to my little Amy I will ask no more."

"Never mind, Geraldine," I answered, "it is not all so bitter as you think it is, and God, who is merciful, will not chastise forever."

"I don't expect peace in this world, but hope for it hereafter," was her reply; "but," she continued, "this has been the brightest hour to me that I have had for many, many years."

We had continued our conversation for some time, and as it was getting late, I arose to go, promising to return often and often to cheer the sinking heart of my poor cousin Geraldine. As I passed through the yard, little Amy, who was waiting for me among the flowers, came to say good-bye. I raised her up in my arms, and said;

"Amy, kiss your cousin."

She looked at me with an amazed expression on her face, and asked:

"My cousin?"

"Yes," I replied, "your cousin and friend."

CHAPTER XVII.

PAUL HEARS BAD NEWS.

THERE was much in this new relationship that gave me pleasure and them comfort; so Geraldine said, who had now some one to advise with. She had indeed found a friend who would be true to her, and this she full well knew. I paid frequent visits to the cottage, and Paul was generally my companion. Eleanor preferred that Gerald should not go, so he was rarely one of the party. How often Geraldine and I would sit in the vine clad piazza and watch Paul and Amy at play. The girl just tall enough to play hide-and-seek over the rose bushes, while the boy would catch her in his strong arms and carry her about from place to place, inventing everything he could for her amusement; and then I would stroke the kitten, and tell them stories, and enjoy seeing them so happy. On one of these evening visits, Geraldine and I were sitting on the porch in our accustomed place, watching the children fly a kite, as Nita and I had done in days gone by. I could scarcely keep from sighing as I looked at them, for we were just as happy once, our voices just as merry, and our smiles as bright. Could they be always children? I said to myself. Heaven forbid that the boy's lot should be like mine.

"John, don't you think Amy a very lovely little thing?" asked Geraldine with all the mother's pride in voice and look.

"Indeed, I do," I said, as we saw her fly through the yard, watching her kite, "and how well matched they are," pointing to Paul.

"Yes, they are," was her reply, "and I often wish that in times to come it may be as it is now, but," she said, and the sad light came again into her eyes, "I cannot define it; in the future there seems to be looming up something which will destroy all. I don't like to think of the future," she continued; "there is no pleasure in it, and there is less in the past."

"But, my dear Geraldine," I began, when I was interrupted by the opening of the little wicket gate, and I saw the man I had met under the firs, Godfrey Laughton. He advanced smiling and bowing in his usual manner; in his path was little Amy, whom he picked up and kissed on her rosy cheeks. The act was nothing more than I would have done myself, but still I was not altogether pleased when I saw it. He came upon the porch and sat down with us, and made his conversation pleasant and affable, but kept his head slightly turned from us, an action which seemed natural with him, but which prevented us from catching his eye whilst he was talking.

Geraldine, when he addressed her, merely answered in monosyllables, and I noticed that she slightly shuddered as he stepped upon the piazza. After a while he asked for Captain Wayland.

"I do not know where he is," said Geraldine, a little nervously, but scarcely had she uttered the words when he joined us. He offered me his hand which I took, and then made room for him to pass; he nodded carelessly to Laughton, and then seated himself on a bench and commanded the old woman Nellie, whom he espied through the windows, to bring him a drink, for he was as thirsty as a deer. He then made some few remarks about the weather. A few moments after, the two men rose, as if by mutual consent, and left us. Godfrey Laughton bowed and bade us good evening, and they walked down the path together. After watching their retreating figures, I turned to Geraldine, who had been also watching them with every vestige of color from her face.

"Do you know," she said, laying her hand upon my arm, "that that man," pointing her finger to Laughton, "has never done me a known injury, but from my very heart I abhor him?"

This was the strongest expression I ever knew, before or after, Geraldine Wayland to make; and this man's visit seemed to have left such a gloomy impression upon her that I did my utmost to remove it, but without much apparent success.

Nothing else of moment occurred for some time, and everything seemed to be growing brighter for Geraldine. One day I got a note from her asking me to come to see her. I went immediately, fearing that there might be something wrong, but when I arrived at the cottage all appeared as usual, and I found my haste to have been unnecessary. After I had been there some time she turned to me and asked:

"John, how long have we known each other?"

"Let me see," I said musingly. "I believe about five years."

"Then my little Amy is entering her twelfth year. Here read this," and she placed in my hand a delicate scented envelope.

I took out the folded paper and read

"DEAR GERALDINE:

"Do not again refuse me the request I made last year and a year or two previous, to let me have my little namesake, Amy. I again renew the promise I have before made, and am more anxious now than ever to have the little darling. I cannot forget our girlhood, dear Geraldine, nor your unvarying kindness to me, and knowing how unhappily you are situated, I am more desirous than ever before to prove my gratitude to you by educating little Amy. Beside, it will be the greatest of pleasures to have her with me. Now, begging you once more not to refuse me,

"I am, as ever, your devoted cousin,
"AMY ST. CLAIR."

"Who is she?" I asked, folding up the letter and replacing it in its envelope.

"She was Amy Oswald, my first cousin, and the only one of my family who wrote to me, or I suppose thought of me, after my marriage."

"Does she live in Paris?" I asked, as I saw the postmark of the letter.

"Oh, no!" she said, "but her husband is very wealthy, and during a portion of the year she resides there. What do you think I had best do?"

"I would advise you to send her by all means," I replied, thinking of her brutal father and the miserable opportunity she had of an education.

"'Twill be a sad blow to me," she said, "to give her up, for she is my only comfort; but when I think of what a great advantage it will be to her, and know, too, that Amy St. Clair will be a second mother to her, I feel that duty requires me to let her go. None will know how I will miss my darling child," she went on, "but I have had so many heartaches already, that nothing seems very hard to bear now; but should anything happen my poor child while she is away from me, how could I ever get to her?"

"Never mind that, Geraldine, I answered; "I promised to be your friend years ago, and I will always keep my pledge."

She understood the significance of these words and held out her hand, whilst grateful tears gathered in her eyes. I clasped the extended hand warmly, and told her that I would come again the next day and assist her in making all the necessary preparations.

As I took my way homeward I could not help feeling very sorry for poor Geraldine, who could not enjoy in peace the one comfort that God had given her. When I reached the Lodge, I found Paul sitting under one of the trees in the yard studying his philosophy. I went up and took a seat by him, and asked him if he had missed his lesson.

"Oh! no, sir," he answered, quickly. "I was only studying this lesson for to-morrow, so that I would have time this evening to go with you to the cottage."

"Yes, Paul, I want you to go with me as often as possible in the next ten days, and see as much of Amy as you can."

"Why?" he asked, looking up into my face somewhat astonished.

"Because she is going away."

"Going away! why, where, uncle?"

"Going to France, my boy, to be gone some several years."

I did not know that this announcement would have had such an effect upon him. He said no more, but his face changed color, and during the rest of the day he was silent and gloomy. I walked with him again that evening to the cottage, and was very much surprised upon reaching it to see a carriage and pair drawn up before the door. We seated ourselves upon the piazza, not wishing to disturb the visitor. I knew it must be a lady from the soft musical tones that reached my ears every now and then, and, at one time, I overheard her say:

"Now, little Amy, when you want a friend you know whom to apply to."

And again:

"Don't be fretting yourself about your mamma, for I am here to take care of her, and whenever she wants you, you shall come back to her."

Shortly after this I heard the rustling of a silk dress, and the lady came to the door followed by Geraldine and Amy. As she stepped on the piazza, Geraldine introduced me to Lady Grantly. She bowed very graciously, made two or three pleasant remarks, kissed Amy most affectionately, and I then assisted her to her carriage, in which she was soon driven out of sight, leaving a very agreeable impression upon me. She was not pretty, but then there was something so superior about her that I felt unconsciously attracted towards her.

Geraldine told me afterwards that she was a good friend of hers, and that would have been enough of itself to ingratiate her in my favor. After this we had a very pleasant chat, and Geraldine insisted that we should stay to tea; every evening of the next week we spent at the cottage. At last the day arrived for Amy's departure. I could scarcely repress a tear myself when I saw her trunk packed and labelled Paris, feeling how many changes would take place, during the years to pass, before I could see her pretty face again. I feared to think of them, for I knew they would be many and great. Poor Geraldine, I never was as sorry for her as I was that morning. It seemed as if she could not give up her only child; the expression of agony in her pale face was so great that it was painful to look upon, and I turned away. At last she was compelled to bid her mother the final adieu as time was pressing, and I took her from the arms of her mother, sobbing as if her little heart would break, and we left Geraldine alone in the cottage with an almost broken heart. Amy had kissed Paul too, who did not attempt to restrain his tears, for his heart was really touched, and he was very, very lonely after the little girl left.

Her father was the last person she came to in bidding us all farewell, and she turned to him saying:

"Good-bye, papa."

"Good-bye, little Amy," he said, and leaned over

and kissed her, and I thought, for the first time, I saw a soft look in his eyes, which seemed to melt his hard face. We then placed her in the carriage and shut the door, waving our hands and handkerchiefs to her till she was out of sight. I returned to the cottage, to the poor, weeping mother, and to Paul, who also needed comfort.

CHAPTER XVIII.

PAUL AND GERALD'S RETURN.

I MAY as well pass over a period of seven years here, for very little occurred in all that time that is worth writing about for the entertainment of any of my readers. It is true that in that time we had sent our boys to college, and I need not say that we missed them sadly. With this exception everything went on in its usual routine, my daily visits to Geraldine, my weekly visits to Paul, and little contentions now and then with Eleanor was the way my life was spent; but now there was coming a great change, the boys were coming back, boys no longer, but young men. Paul was a graduate with the highest honors. Gerald was not so fortunate. Eleanor attributed this to ill-health, but I attributed it to its real cause, inferiority of mind. I could see each day that Eleanor was jealous of Paul's progress, and when she heard with what honor and distinction he had graduated, she turned away wholly displeased. It was already Thursday evening in June, and the following day the boys were to be at home. I was so anxious to see Paul, that all the evening I was restless and walking about at random. Eleanor came out and met me as I came upon the piazza, and joined me in my promenade.

"I declare, John," she said, "I can scarcely wait until to-morrow to see Gerald, I am so anxious to see him. Lord Gordon," she said, addressing her husband, who was smoking a cigar at the upper end of the balcony, and watching his dogs gamboling on the lawn, "has Gerald improved any, you have seen him since I have?"

"It won't be long until you can see for yourself, Eleanor, and I would rather you would be the judge. Paul is a handsome fellow, John, and he has such a fine address."

"Yes, Paul has given me great satisfaction, and I am justly proud of him, a worthy descendant of the House of Graham," I said, looking at Eleanor, thinking that this would please her, for she was proud of her family; but she turned away her head, seemingly very much provoked, and said to Lord Gordon:

"It is strange that you never see anything in your own son that is worthy of praise or admiration."

"Indeed I do, my wife," he said, looking at her proudly, for she was still a very beautiful woman; "Gerald's career so far has pleased me greatly, especially as he has always been so weak and delicate." Here he gave a significant glance at me.

She seemed to be satisfied after this, and the rest of the evening passed pleasantly enough. We all retired early anxious for the night to be over that we could meet the dawning of the coming day, which arrived at last bright and cheering. I was awakened early by the chattering of the birds outside on the limbs of the trees, and by a sunbeam which stole in through an aperture in the shutter, and fell across my eyes. I jumped up hurriedly, remembering the day, and went down to an early breakfast, for everyone seemed like myself, anxious to be up and doing. We chatted away pleasantly enough during breakfast; Eleanor looking at her watch twenty times during the meal, to see when the hour would come that would bring her son. "Well, Eleanor," I asked, "how many hours now before they will be here."

"I don't know," she said, laughing. "I believe my watch has run down, the hands don't seem to have changed position since I looked at it last."

"I suppose not," said Lord Gordon, smiling; "for you havn't given them time."

We all three laughed at this, and then adjourned to the sitting room which overlooked the carriage road. I drew a comfortable chair to the window, and looked out upon the scenery around. Everything seemed to be lazily sleeping beneath the warm rays of the June sun; even the great sea appeared slumbering, so idly and slowly it was flowing along with the sunbeams kissing its surface. But I was not thinking of all this; my thoughts were with the boys that were coming back, and were now not far from us. I offered an inward prayer that their manhood would be spent more agreeably together than their childhood. My heart was right heavy on that day, when it should have been so light, and as I turned to the centre table near which Eleanor was sitting, leaning over a piece of fancy work, I sighed heavily, for there was the same face, the face of Eleanor Graham, beautiful still, but cold and stern and unsoftened by years, or by trouble either, for in Eleanor's vocabulary this little word was missing. I turned again to the window and waited patiently for the next half hour to elapse, but I had not waited more than twenty minutes, when I saw two young horsemen cantering along the moorland road; my heart beat high, for I knew but too well who these were. As they came up without breaking their lope to the Lodge gate, joyfully opened by the old porter, one of them leaned his graceful figure forward and shook the old man's hand cordially, whilst the other gave a careless nod and came rapidly onwards, and was soon in the arms of his mother. I shook Gerald warmly by both hands, welcoming him back to the Lodge, and then hastened to meet Paul, who jumped from his horse, and ran forward to meet me.

"My noble boy!"

"My dear uncle!"

He was then clasped in my arms; at length I pushed him from me to take a survey of his person, and a nobler form, or a manlier face had rarely met my eyes.

"Paul, I am really proud of you."

"I have worked hard to make you so, uncle," whilst a slight blush of pleasure suffused his cheek.

"Bless you, my boy," I returned, as I led the way up the steps.

Eleanor gave him her hand, saying, "How are you Paul?"

"Very well, Aunt Eleanor, and am glad to see looking so well," he answered, as he shook her hand.

"Oh, yes, I am feeling very well, thank you," and this was all. But Lord Gordon was much more cordial; he met Paul, saying:

"Well, Paul, we are delighted to see you back, and many times welcome to Gordon; you are an honor to us all, old fellow, and we are proud of you."

"Oh, thank you," said Paul, his color brightening. "You honor me too much by saying this."

"Honor to whom honor is due, you know," replied Lord Gordon, and we walked to the sitting room, where Eleanor and Gerald had preceded us, and took our seats.

Eleanor was seated upon the sofa with her arms around Gerald, whose head rested upon her shoulder; it was still a fair head, with an abundance of light curls clustering about the blue-veined forehead; the expression of the face was rather effeminate, and there was little about it that denoted character, strength, or vigor. His hand was as white and delicate as that of his mother's, which he was holding, calling her all the while by a dozen pet names, and telling her that all England would never make him stay so long away from her again, and saying, laughing:

"I have not felt so much at home for the last six years."

"Nor I so happy, my son," said his mother; "and you certainly are not going away from me again; it is too great a pain to be separated from you."

And she looked at him with the old look of tenderness, which her face wore whilst gazing upon her son, and which I never saw there at any other time.

And there they sat, he coaxing and scolding by turns, in a half-boyish way, for not bringing him home before, and saying that she was "never to let him go away again, and that there was nobody in this world like his pretty mamma."

Thus they carried on their conversation, whilst we sat some distance apart, speaking of various things, while Lord Gordon sat at an equal distance between the two, speaking first to his wife and then to his son. In the course of our conversation, Paul asked me about Amy and when she was coming. I answered by asking him if he remembered her.

"Indeed I do," he said, "just as well as if it had been yesterday we parted."

"I suppose she will be at home some time this summer; at least Geraldine was hoping this when I saw her last."

He was looking out the window whilst I was speaking, and happening to see his old dog, he exclaimed:

"If there is not my old dog, looking just as well as ever! I do wonder if he would know me?"

I bade him lean forward and see. He did as he was bid, saying:

"Come here, old fellow."

The dog, as he recognized the old familiar tones, lifted his head, wagged his tail, and whined with delight. Again Paul called:

"Come here, Warder."

The dog jumped up, with two or three bounds reached the piazza, put his great paws upon the window-sill and his nose almost in his master's face, and then leaped about and barked so furiously that he almost deafened us, whilst Paul, to quiet him, stroked and patted him upon the head. The rest of the time the faithful animal was content to lie under the window and watch his master's every movement.

"Well, old boy" (this was Paul's usual manner of addressing him), "you would be a good teacher to many a fickle one in this world by your constancy and faithfulness."

There were so many questions to be asked and answered, so many anecdotes to be told, and so many servants to be spoken to who came to welcome their young masters, that we found the day had almost passed before we knew it and night coming on. Eleanor entertained her son after tea with a few songs, for her voice was still good, and at half after ten, the boys being tired, we all arose, bade each other good night, and sought our separate chambers. This was a very pleasant beginning, and I trusted it would continue so unto the end.

The next evening Paul asked me if I would not walk with him to the cottage to see Geraldine. I answered "With all my heart," and we took our hats and went forth along the old familiar road which we had trod years before when he was but a boy. But now he walked beside me almost as tall as myself, noble and graceful, and true to his manhood in every sense of the word. He was as unaffected as he was when a boy, and our conversation was as easy and unrestrained as it was then. As we neared the cottage everything had a cheery and brighter appearance than it had worn for these many years, when the little girl's silvery laugh rang out in the yard and the little footsteps never tired of pattering down the piazza. Though the laugh was quiet and the sound of the footstep I could not hear, still there were the parlor windows open and the muslin curtains, pure and white as the snowdrift, pushed back upon their brackets, while the canary (a worthy descendant of the one that hung there so many years ago) carolled away in half sleepy notes a sweet melody. The whole aspect of the cottage seemed to have undergone a change, and my curiosity was excited to know the reason. As we reached the foot of the step, Geraldine came out on the piazza to meet us, with her sad face looking brighter and happier than I had seen it look for many a long day. Closely following her was a young girl of apparently some eighteen or nineteen summers, whom I instantly recognized as Amy, clothed in a pretty, cool summer muslin, with a pink rose nestling in her soft brown curls. I do not think I ever beheld a fairer picture than she represented as she held out her two small hands to us, exclaiming in the softest and pleasantest accents:

"What a charming meeting! How delighted I am to see you!"

"Of course I knew you, Paul," she said, in answer to his enquiry if she would have recognized him if he had come unaccompanied by me. "Of course you have grown and have changed too a great deal, but there is something about you that I would have recognized, though I do not know what it is."

"You know," she went on in a lively strain, "I have always considered you a hero, and you must have impressed me very forcibly when you rescued my kitten, and me too, from a watery grave."

"Oh, yes," he answered, "I remember all that, and hope I won't lose all claim to that appellation, but hope too that you will allow me to render you many a service."

"Indeed I will, whenever an opportunity presents itself," she said, laughing, "but I hope you do not want me to fall into the sea again."

"No, not you," he answered, "but I would not mind your kitten falling in, so that I might prove to you that I am a true knight."

Thus they were chatting away happily and freely, when my surprise was awakened to its fullest as I saw Gerald open the cottage gate and enter. He was invited into the parlor by Geraldine and introduced to her daughter. Scarcely had he taken his seat than he was followed by another visitor, and I thought it a most disagreeable intrusion when I recognized Godfrey Laughton. Geraldine and I sat apart watching this group of four, and I saw that Laughton was instantly struck with Amy's beauty and the simplicity of her manners. I saw too that he was determined to win her, and was then using all his powers of fascination to attract her; and Gerald's susceptible heart was easily made captive; while Paul, who had loved her always, seemed to have that same faithfulness and constancy which he the day before admired so much in his dog.

I thought I noticed a little fear and a shrinking from Godfrey in Amy, and she seemed to observe, as I did long before, the restlessness in his eye and the unquietness in his manner. To Gerald she appeared somewhat indifferent, to my scrutinizing glance, though to another observer she would have appeared altogether attentive. I did not mark the impression that Paul had made upon her, though I am very sure it must have been an agreeable one, for otherwise I would have noticed it. I think she tried to conceal as much as possible her feelings and to treat the three gentlemen with the same degree of cordiality.

The evening was very far advanced when we left the cottage to return home. Godfrey Laughton, whom we had left behind, shortly after joined us, saying:

"As my home lies in this direction, it will give me great pleasure to accompany you all that far."

"We will be pleased to have you," we all said in a voice, and silence for a few moments ensued, which was broken by Gerald saying:

"I think Amy Wayland is adorable!"

"Ah! indeed!" returned Laughton. "So your heart is taken captive already?"

"Oh! I do not think it is as bad as that," he said, laughing; "but she is truly very charming, and I will acknowledge that it is in danger."

"What do you think of her, Mr. Steuart?" Laughton asked, patting Paul upon the shoulder. "Are you as far gone as Sir Gerald?"

I thought Paul a little offended at the rather light tones in which they spoke of Amy, for I had taught him all my life to venerate the fair sex, of whom he had a most exalted opinion; and though he had not loved Amy, I think he would have been equally offended.

"My opinion of *Miss Wayland* is a very high one,"

he said. "I think her a most charming young lady, and I admire her character even more than I do her face."

"Oh!" said Laughton, with quite a sinister sneer, "I think you quite as much, if not more, enchanted than Sir Gerald!"

"Do you?" was the cool reply, and the subject was not renewed again.

At the place of parting, as we were shaking hands with Godfrey, he said:

"I hope you gentlemen will join my fishing excursion on next Thursday and dine with me at 'Merry Hall.'"

Gerald gladly accepted the invitation, but Paul slightly hesitated, when Laughton said:

"I will take no excuse from you, Mr. Steuart," and waved his hand in adieu.

CHAPTER XIX.

THE FISHING EXCURSION.

THE morning of the fishing party soon arrived. Paul seemed still to hesitate about going, when I asked him after breakfast, but I insisted upon it, for he was still a hard student, and I was anxious for him to take as much recreation as possible. He allowed himself but little, a walk to the cottage in the evening and an occasional hunt with his old dog being all, as he was just as fond of bringing down a bird as anybody, and the old dog seemed just as delighted at seeing his master with his gun as he was long ago when he was young and full of life and strength.

"You seem determined that I shall go," said Paul, laughing, "and as you wish it so earnestly, I will certainly comply."

So in about an hour or two afterwards the boys started. I watched the two graceful figures out of sight, and then took my accustomed seat on the verandah with my book, and Warder, with his nose at my feet, dozing in the sun.

I was not an eye-witness to the occurrences of this chapter, but will relate them in the exact words in which they were told to me by a truthful and impartial witness.

The young men reached "Merry Hall" a short time after leaving the Lodge. They were received in a most hospitable manner by the host, who ushered them into a large, airy drawing-room, where the company were assembled, entirely composed of gentlemen, and apparently much at their ease, some lounging on velvet divans puffing away at cigars, and others formed into parties of cribbage, whist, and backgammon, stopping occasionally in their games to drink the health, in the choicest wine, of the prettiest girls in the country.

"Why, gentlemen," he said, as the three entered the drawing-room together, "I had nearly come to the conclusion that we were to be deprived of your delightful society to-day; and these gentlemen," pointing to the loungers and players, "as well as myself were bemoaning our fate most piteously."

"Oh! as for me," answered Gerald, "I have been ready for an age, but this young man here," touching Paul, "is a fearful procrastinator."

"Yes," said Paul, smiling pleasantly, "I suppose I am in fault here, if there is any blame to be attached, for I was having a chat with my uncle, which detained me longer than I was aware of."

"Paul seems to be making a virtue of necessity in having these daily conversations."

A dark frown contracted the young man's face thus spoken of, and his eyes flashed as he turned to make a retort, but his attention was arrested by an exclamation from one of the chess players.

"Why, Steuart, my boy, is it possible!"

"Why, Leigh, well met! Where did you come from? Just from the tombs?"

"Do I look so ghostly?" replied the other, laughing.

"No, not at all; but if I had seen the spirit of my grandfather I could not have been more surprised."

"Perhaps I can make you think of the spirit of your grandmother too," said Leigh, as he pointed to a table where four young men were engaged at a rubber of whist.

"Well, as I live!" exclaimed Paul, "if there ain't Anthony Gay! A *gay* meeting, truly," he continued, punning on the name.

"And a gay scene," said Leigh, "for a gay boy is Gay."

"Yes," said Anthony, whose attention was attracted from his game by hearing his name called so often, as he sprang from the table with both hands extended to Paul, "and we are going to have a gay time of it, boys, for the sight of you has made my heart as gay and light as a bird's," and he broke out singing the first two or three stanzas from Traviata:

> "Gaily, gaily through life wander,
> Cloud not our existence with care," &c.

"That's right, my friends," said Godfrey, coming up. "It is better to laugh than be sighing, and now whilst I think of it, life's moments are flying very rapidly and we had better be away to the Isles, or I fear the fish will be taking an after dinner's nap before we can get to them." He looked at his watch, and said: "I will have the horses ordered," and left them.

The three young men were still standing in the floor laughing and talking, when they were somewhat startled by champagne corks flying in close proximity to their heads, and turning they saw a party of about seven with sparkling wine cups raised to their lips, whilst a voice, which Paul knew but too well, was saying:

"I propose a toast to old Wayland's daughter, the prettiest girl in the country O!"

The young man hearing this, gritted his teeth, and shrugged his shoulders.

"You don't belong to that party, Steuart?" asked Gay, as he nodded towards the seven.

"No," said Paul, emphatically, shaking his head.

"Nor you, Leigh?" continued Gay, addressing the other.

"Not I, indeed, sir," he returned, playfully.

"Then as I think you are two of the best fellows I ever met, I shall join your standard, and we shall call ourselves "The Thirsty Three," for I must say it is a dry society you belong to."

"Here, give me your hand, Anthony," said Paul, "for you are a man after my own heart."

"A worthy son of a worthy sire," added the third, as he too held out his hand to Anthony.

"And proud to be the friend of the worthy Steuart, and the worthy Leigh," he answered, as he shook warmly both the extended hands.

The announcement was then made that all was ready, and they wended their way to the sea where their little boats, whose sails had just been hoisted, were waiting to receive them; it was not long before they were fairly launched on the waters, and many a net was thrown in the water to entrap the unsuspecting fish beneath.

"I have caught the whale, boys," said Anthony, as he brought in a huge sea turtle; "I am going to send it to my Aunt Grantly to-morrow with my love, and tell her I am going to help her make her Friday dinner off of it. And did you all hear the news," he said, turning to Paul and Leigh. "She is going to give a fancy ball for her airy, fairy Lillian, and I suppose it is to be her turning-out affair, and we are to have the jolly set of merry Andrews there," slapping a young man on the shoulders who had just brought in a huge salmon, and who all the boys called Andy. "And I can tell you who else is to be there," he continued; "that pretty little daughter of Captain Wayland's, and I tell you what it is, she's a beauty; and I'll tell you something else too, that chap over there, Gerald Gordon, is as much in love with her as he knows how to be, but he don't know how much, and what he does know will be too much for his mother, for that boy must marry a princess, nothing else will do her."

"Poor princess," said Leigh, amused, whilst Paul leaned over and played with the water, looking somewhat sad, but he was too cheerful to look that way long, and he soon after turned to Anthony, and said:

"Well, Gay, any more news?"

"No, nothing else, only you came mighty near tumbling into the water just now, and when I caught you, saying, 'look out Steuart, you'll be drowned,' you said, 'No matter.' Do you know what you were thinking about; if you don't, I do: you were thinking about catching a fish and could not. Now let me tell you, for your consolation, what you must have heard ever since you were born, 'that there are as good fish in the sea as ever were caught.'"

"Well, gayest of the Gay," said Paul, laughing, "if it will be any satisfaction to you, I am consoled."

"If you are, I'm not, and won't be until I get my dinner, for I'm awfully hungry; and how is it with you, Walter?" he asked, turning to Lord Leigh.

"I don't know how *it is*," answered Leigh, "until I see what I have got here," tugging away at his net.

"I suppose *it is*, that you would like me to give you a lift," said Anthony, winking roguishly, and stretching forth his strong arm.

"Anthony, you are the greatest case in all England," replied Leigh, good-humoredly, as our boat touched the island. Here Godfrey Laughton jumped from the boat, and made a graceful speech inviting the boys to land, and leading them to a tastefully erected bower, where a sumptuous repast was spread. They were all soon, as Anthony expressed it, "hauling in dinner instead of fish." After refreshing themselves sufficiently, Paul and Walter Leigh walked off to a shady part of the island, and threw themselves upon the ground to have a friendly tete-a-tete. They had been college friends and were still heart whole, though we would not like to say fancy free, could we have heard the frequent mention of Amy, and the airy, fairy Lillian (as Anthony has justly styled her) which they made. They had been lounging there for an hour, when Paul was interrupted by one of the party, calling, "Steuart, you are wanting, come quickly."

"Who wants me?"

"Gordon is in danger," answered the man, "and Anthony Gay has sent for you."

Paul leaped to his feet and hastened to the spot, followed by Lord Leigh, and found there two men ready for a duel, one, the heir of Gordon, the other, Godfrey Laughton.

"What are you going to do," Paul asked, as he came to Gerald's side.

"Kill Laughton," was the short answer.

"And this is the return you make for hospitality received," said Paul, a little contemptuously.

"Go away, and attend to your own business," cried Gerald, in an excited and intoxicated voice; "I shall do as I please."

"Not this time," said Paul, firmly, taking the pistol out of his nervous, trembling hand. "Sit down and make a man of yourself, no one but a coward fights a duel."

These words seemed to appease Gerald, and Paul raised his voice, saying:

"I'll leave it to the party. Are these gentlemen fit subjects for dueling?"

"And I answer in the name of all," said Lord Leigh, "and say that they *are not.*"

"And I, and I, and I," said a dozen others.

"Then seconds your services are no longer needed," Paul said, addressing the gentlemen who had volunteered this office.

Laughton was not so easily gained over as Gerald and was actually foaming with rage; but at length Paul, by persuasion and firmness, succeeded in quieting him.

"A brave man is that Steuart," said one of the party to a companion.

"Faith, that he is," he answered. "I would not interfere with Godfrey Laughton when excited for the world, for I would know that my life would be in jeopardy. But as for that Steuart, I don't believe he'd be afraid of the old fellow himself."

As they were preparing to leave the island, Paul inquired of Anthony Gay the cause of the disagreement.

"I don't know, exactly" he answered; "but that old Wayland's daughter was at the bottom of it."

"And," remarked one of the by-standers, "'tis my opinion that she will be at the bottom of many another one."

CHAPTER XX.

PAUL MAKES A CONFESSION.

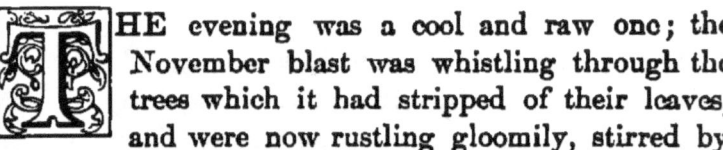HE evening was a cool and raw one; the November blast was whistling through the trees which it had stripped of their leaves, and were now rustling gloomily, stirred by its chilling blast. There were bright fires burning in the library and parlor, and throughout the whole Lodge an air of comfort prevailed.

I threw my cloak over my shoulders and walked to Geraldine's, but found them all absent. I learned that Amy was out riding with Gerald notwithstanding the inclemency of the evening.

"Gerald," said Nellie, "had insisted upon her going and would take no excuse, for the engagement had been made some days before, and Geraldine had gone to visit a poor peasant woman who had a very sick child, to offer consolation."

I retraced my steps homeward through the woods, crushing the sered leaves as I went, with the winds every now and then playing bandy with my hat, till I was compelled to use my hands, which I placed on the top of my head, and then bade them defiance. When I reached the Lodge, I hung my cloak and hat upon the rack in the Hall and walked into the Library. There sat Paul in the gloaming before the cheerful grate, his large dog beside him with his head upon his master's knee, looking into his face with his fond old eyes. The boy had just been on a hunt, for the game bag was thrown carelessly over a chair, and his gun was as carelessly leaning against the table.

"Well, what luck," I said, rubbing my hands.

"As usual, uncle," he answered, rising, and offering me a chair.

"Don't get up, Paul, here is a very comfortable chair," and I drew a large arm chair near the fire.

He resumed his old position, still watching the blaze. I sat slightly apart looking at the face that the flickering light fell upon; it was usually so bright, so cheering, always lighted by a winsome smile; but what was the matter this evening? what was the meaning of that half frown, that sad look, would my boy tell me? I asked the question inwardly. I drew my chair near the table by which he was sitting, and asked:

"What ails you, my son?"

He started, and blushed slightly; then looking at me affectionately, said:

"Why, what could be the matter with me, uncle I am just as well as I ever was."

"You are as well in body; but is that all, Paul?"

"Why, uncle, I am sure that is enough, when a man is well in body he should be well in every other respect."

"There is something you are keeping from me, Paul, and is this like you to withhold from me your confidence?"

He got up, and stood with his back to the fire, and said, hurriedly:

"For pity sake, uncle, don't think I am withholding anything from you that I ought to tell, for don't you know you are master of every secret of my life which is of the least importance."

He then feared he had spoken to me too hurriedly, came up to me and took my hand in both of his, and caressed it, saying:

"This is the hand that guided me through life, that steadied my infant steps, directed those of my boyhood, and brought me into manhood; and can I be a traitor to its guidance by concealing anything?"

He then sat down and told me of his love for Amy, how he feared it would all be foiled, for another, more favored by fortune, seemed to be superceding him in her affections.

"But," he said, rising to his feet, and the old smile of cheerfulness striving to take possession of his face, "I ought to be a man, and stand it like one, and not be troubling your kind, old heart with a school-boy affair, *and I will be a man too,*" he repeated, in that tone of firmness for which he was remarkable.

"Don't think it a weakness, my child, to love a true, good woman; but, perhaps, Paul, your love is not so hopelessly bestowed as you imagine. I think I know little Amy better than you do, and as a word to the wise is sufficient, I will merely say that it is not a woman's place to make advances."

I think he was much comforted by the time our conversation ended, and he was just as determined, if Amy loved him to fight a battle to obtain her, as he had been in all the other affairs of life, to win. So, throughout the winter and the following spring, his attentions to her were untiring, and I noticed that the girl's face was more smiling and her eyes brighter than they had been since she was a little girl.

One day, in the following spring, after Paul and myself had returned home from a visit to an old friend, we were sitting in the drawing-room at the Lodge. Gerald had been out all morning, and I was told he had gone to the cottage. When he returned about dinner time, his mother rose to greet him, asking:

"Why where have you been, my darling, you are a perfect truant?"

"Oh! I have been here, there, and everywhere, mamma, it would be hard to say."

"Well, can't you just tell me one of the places, for I would like to know how you do entertain yourself when you are away?"

"Let me see," he began; "I was at Lady Grantley's for a little while, and heard that young Countess, who is paying a visit to the pretty Lillian, chatter away, and sing some favorite airs from Lucia de Lammermoor and Norma, and some other operas that I didn't care anything about. I then went to Laughton's to learn when our next hunting party would come off."

After this, Gerald remained silent, when Paul asked, a little spitefully:

"How did you leave them all the cottage, Gerald?" seeing that Gerald was not going to acknowledge his visit there.

Eleanor, whose face was wreathed in smiles, now reddened, and she said angrily:

"My son does not visit the cottage."

"I am sorry you do not know your son as well as I do," Paul retorted.

"What do you mean by this, sir," said Gerald, rising, whilst the veins in his temple were swollen with anger.

"Merely what my words contained. If you are ashamed to acknowledge your visit to a lady and to a lady's house, I am not ashamed to tell it for you."

"No matter where my son visits, sir," put in Eleanor, "it is not your place to bring him to an account for it, and you shall never do it again."

"That was not my intention, madam," said Paul, equally provoked, and rising from the sofa upon which he was lounging, "but I say when a man is ashamed to say that he visits a lady that he does visit, that man's intentions are dishonorable, and that he is not a gentleman."

He then left the room to walk upon the piazza to cool his temper, for temper was his great fault, and I was not surprised to see him a little while after take his hat and walk away in the direction of the cottage.

That evening later, when I saw two forms walking along the beach—a graceful girl and a noble-looking man—I felt that all was going well; and when Paul returned that night and told me simply that he had asked her to be his wife, and that she, with all a woman's confidence, had given him her love, I thanked God for making the boy so happy; the sky seemed so peaceful and tranquilly bright, for our hearts were at peace.

CHAPTER XXI.

JOHN MAKES A GREAT MISTAKE.

I TOLD Eleanor in a day or two our secret. Perhaps it was not advisable in me to have done so, but I thought it was nothing more than my duty, as she was the only female relative that Paul had, and she should have stood to him in the light of a mother. I thought, too, that it would ease her mind as regarded Gerald, for she was making herself very miserable about him, for fear he would fall in love with Amy. I heard him tell her one day, when they had some words about her, that if he chose he would marry her anyhow; that she could not prevent him, nor his father either. When I told her of Paul's engagement, there was an expression in her face which for the first time in my life I failed to understand; and I noticed that during the following days she was colder, if possible, in her manners to Paul, and she still wore the expression that I did not understand.

I remember one day, whilst sitting in the front verandah, that I noticed Amy's graceful figure coming towards the Lodge. I had scarcely time to be surprised at this when she reached the foot of the stairs, saying:

"Good morning, uncle" (for she always called me that). "Why ain't you up and about this glorious day? Why, the very birds seem to be inviting you forth."

"I suppose you are on pleasure bent?" I answered, taking her hand.

"No,"—shaking her head and smiling significantly. "If I were on that you would not think I would turn my steps in this direction, would you?"

"No," I replied, smiling too, and waited for an explanation.

"I came to see Lady Gordon. Is she at home?"

"Come in, then, and I will have her here in a few minutes."

I rang for a servant, and told him to tell Lady Gordon that Miss Wayland was waiting to see her.

The domestic bowed and left, and in a few moments Eleanor appeared. She greeted Amy most cordially (which much surprised me), and took a seat beside her on the sofa. I was not a little delighted and pleased to see with what perfect ease and grace little Amy chatted away to this Lady Gordon whom so many held in awe. After awhile she told Eleanor that she had come on a very charitable expedition; that both she and Lillian Grantly had been authorized to go about and collect alms for several poor families who had been burnt out of house and home the night previous, and who were now in actual destitution. Any assistance that Lady Gordon would render would be most thankfully received.

"I will most gladly assist you," Eleanor answered, with more warmth than she had used for years; "but pray, Miss Wayland, sit longer," as Amy rose to go.

"No, thank you, Lady Gordon, my mission is not yet accomplished by any means." Amy then bowed herself out, but not until she had received many repeated invitations to visit the Lodge frequently.

I walked out with her, down the lawn to the Lodge gate. When we had gone about twenty yards, she turned to me and said:

"Can you tell me why Lady Gordon was so very gracious to me this morning?"

"God knows, my child," I answered, feeling anything but easy as I thought about it.

We walked on then a moment in silence, when I asked:

"Are you going to Lady Grantly's ball?"

"I suppose I must, as Lillian insists upon it, and Paul wishes me to go, too."

"Oh, yes, my child," I said. "I don't see why you should not go, as it is to be a very select party, and I don't know why you should not enjoy yourself as well as other young people."

"I am anxious to go, uncle, and think I will have a very pleasant time."

"Remember, Amy, if there is anything I can help you with you must be sure to let me know."

"Thank you many times," she said, looking at me most affectionately. "Uncle, you are one of my best friends."

"I am very glad you think so, my child, for you are most dear to me."

We had reached the gate, and as I opened it, we saw approaching the fairy Lillian, whose sunny face was wreathed in smiles.

"What!" I said, somewhat surprised as I advanced and shook hands with her, "You walking, too?"

"Of course, I am," she returned, with a merry laugh. "You did not expect me to go on charitable missions in a carriage, did you? Why, such indolence would make the angels weep."

"That you will never do," I replied, holding the small hand.

"Oh! you don't know. I am very naughty sometimes. If you had said that to Amy there would have been some truth in it."

"Hush!" said Amy, blushing like a summer rose. "I fear they weep for me very often."

"Not for your faults," returned Lillian; "they only weep to have you with them."

"Because you are a little angel yourself, Lillian, you need not think everybody else follows in your footsteps."

"Well, this is decidedly the most complimentary conversation I ever overheard," exclaimed Lord Leigh, as he sprang lightly over a fence near us, with his gun pon his shoulder and a couple of dogs following him.

"Miss Amy, I must admire your penetration and judgment;" but while he addressed Amy, he looked into the soft blue eyes of the young countess with a depth of love which was not intended for either Amy or I to understand, but under which the pretty little creature blushed and smiled, saying:

"So you have been an eaves-dropper, Walter? It's a wonder you did not hear something about yourself, sir."

"That is what I was listening for," he said, laughing, "but when you commenced about the angels I knew you would never descend to me, so I thought I would come to the angels. But don't you think," he continued, "that it is too warm for you to be standing here in the sun? Come, let me take you home before the sun gets much higher."

There was so much concern and care expressed in his manner towards this young girl, that it called forth unbounded admiration on my part.

He then asked Amy if she were not going in their direction, and if she would not accompany them.

"Oh! no," she answered. "My mission is not yet finished, and then I will have good company anyhow, for uncle is going to accompany me."

"Then, good-bye," both said in a breath, "and be sure," continued Lillian, "to be at the ball on Thursday, Amy. And you, too, Mr. Meredith; remember you are not exempt; we will certainly expect you."

"Yes, that we will, Mr. Meredith," said Lord Leigh, "and you must not fail to be there. And, Mr. Meredith, won't you tell Paul, in his rounds of visits this evening to call to see me? I have something to say to him. He has been a real truant as regards me lately," looking at Amy a little roguishly. "I have an old claim on him, Miss Amy, and I am not going to give him up so easily."

"Not as old as mine, though," said Amy, laughing merrily, and nodding adieu.

CHAPTER XXII.

LADY GRANTLY'S FANCY BALL.

THURSDAY, the night of the ball, came at last. There was a great deal of excitement at the Lodge, for we were all going, but none in costume, except the boys. Eleanor asked me in the evening what my costume was to be.

"That of a gentleman," I answered, bowing gravely, "for it is not necessary for me to assume a character, like it seems to be for the others," I continued, with mock gravity.

We all laughed, and Eleanor told me that I had my share of self-appreciation.

We did not see the boys in their costumes, for they sent us word that they would see us at the ball, and left in the pony carriage before we were quite ready.

Everything was superbly arranged at the Grantly Manor. I felt that I was going into fairyland as I went into the dancing saloons and parlors.

> "Blue spirits in white, red spirits in grey,
> All mingled, mingled, mingled."

There were dashing cavaliers, bold knights, officers, bold marshals, princes, and kings; while beautifully-robed princesses, court ladies, and graceful dames of high degree were dancing, laughing, talking, and chatting with daring brigands, corsairs, fanciful troubadours, country belles, flower girls, nymphs, and fairies. Mrs. Partington and Paul Pry enjoyed a cozy chat on a tete-a-tete sofa, while Paddy flew around in the dance, embracing the Queen of the Amazons. There, too, was Mother Goose and a graceful Varsovienne, with Richard Cœur de Leon; while Meg Merrilles and Madge Wildfire were carrying on sly flirtations with a French grenadier and Sir Walter Raleigh; and German and Roman peasant girls were bandying repartee with Ravenswood and Monte Cristo; while pale, pretty Lucy Ashton was standing apart, talking in a lively strain to Dogberry; and Stradella stood in his velvet mantle, whispering words of love to his Leonora. You could see anywhere groups of Romeos and Juliets, Othellos and Desdemonas, Harlequins, and Merry Andrews in the mazes of the dance, with Helen McGregor, Undines, and even a little Topsy, who was impudent enough to take her place and smile on a fascinating knight. And there was the terrible Katharina still shaking at Petruchio, and vowing that the moon was the sun.

I sat a little apart with some old friends, and gazed with delight on this enchanting scene. I had not as yet seen any of our party, the crowd being so dense; but presently I caught sight of Lillian, and indeed she was an airy fairy in her dress of white gossamer, carrying a beautiful little wand, which she was playfully waving over the head of a Cinderella. I heard many remarks made upon her beauty and simplicity, and really there was much to admire in this lovely character.

My attention was attracted from her to a couple who were walking towards a door which led to the conservatory. I leaned forward to get a better view, but I could not see their faces. The gentleman was attired in the handsome dress of the Knight of St. John, while the girl wore a Greek costume. They passed on through the door, and I did not see them for some time afterwards. Presently I heard the following remarks from some of the bystanders, and as they concerned little Amy, I was all attention.

"They say old Wayland's daughter is here somewhere, and that she is a perfect beauty. But let us find out this Wayland contagion. I want to see her."

"And you will be sure to catch it, like most of the young men to-night. But come on; let us go and be introduced to her."

These two passed out of hearing, but an Eastern princess standing near speaking to a French field-marshal took up the subject.

"I suppose you have seen that very pretty girl, the daughter of old Captain Wayland, whom everybody says is such a case. They live in the cottage that is in that cool, shady grove. It is a pretty place enough I dare say, but so tiny that one would suppose it was made for a doll baby. I am sure I should suffocate had I to live in a place so small. I cannot see for the life of me how people can exist in such small places."

"Yes, it is very distressing," said the other, in what I thought to be a very sneering voice. "I am very sure your Royal Highness could never be content with 'love in a cottage.'"

"Ah! no, indeed; it must be on a larger scale or I never should survive it. But let me beg you, Monsieur, not to be sarcastic."

"Why, no, your Highness, I had no such intention. I do not know the lady in question, but I should like very much to become acquainted with her."

"And that you shall," said a third, stepping up—a knight with a waving plume—"for I myself will introduce you; that is, if I can find her. I have her name down for a set, and must begin my search, for I cannot afford to miss the pleasant opportunity of spending a half hour with so charming a person as Miss Amy."

Then the three walked away, but I did not fail to recognize in the independent gait of the man who had last spoken our old friend, Anthony Gay.

I soon tired of this gay, bright scene, for my spirits were not exactly in keeping with it. So after partaking of the refreshments, I went up stairs to a little harp room which stood at the end of a long corridor; the room was small and prettily arranged, and hung with green damask. The harp was pushed into one corner uncovered, and near it a music stand on which a pile of sheet music was lying. I turned over several of these sheets, and as I came to the last I found an old ballad, "Hours there were to memory dearer." Ah! what did it bring back to me? The remembrance of a voice that was long hushed and at rest, which used, in plaintive tones, to sing this; every word of that old song brought back to me "bright visions of the past." I again, in thought, went over that period of my early manhood, remembering those sunny smiles, and nearly every word those lips had uttered, and as I read this stanza in the song:

"Friends were fonder; joys were nearer;
But, alas! they're passed away."

I laid down the sheet, and passed my hand two or three times over my brow to shut out the visions of years ago. I then walked to the window and drawing back the heavy curtains, took my seat in the deep embrasure, drew the curtains to again, and looked out on the night. The sea was flowing slowly on, silvered by the moon's pale rays, while all around was peaceful and serene, except from below, where I could still hear the strains of music and the dancers' merry feet, and I knew the revelry was still at its height. I was glad to be alone here in this quiet spot, and had determined to enjoy its solitude. I had taken out a cigar with the intention of lighting it, when a slight noise in the room awakened my attention; a couple entered, a lady and a gentleman. When I saw them through a slight opening in the curtain, they were standing, in the centre of the room, at a little table, and he was pouring out for her a glass of water. I saw that it was the Knight of St. John and the Greek girl; but what was my astonishment, when, turning their faces towards me, I recognized Paul and Amy. I don't know why I did not address them, but it seemed to me I had lost the power either to speak or move; perhaps it was the troubled expression I saw in the face of one, and the anxiety depicted on the face of the other that kept me silent. They took a seat on a little velvet divan, and reluctantly I heard the following short conversation:

"Now, Amy, you must tell me what he said to you, for Gerald Gordon is no friend of mine. Perhaps I am more uneasy than may be necessary about all these things, but you are so very dear to me, that it may be this that makes me so."

"I wish I hadn't said anything to you about it, Paul, for you worry yourself so unnecessarily. Don't you know that all Gerald Gordon could say in a lifetime would not affect me, me that you call your dauntless Amy?"

"I know that, but still it is only right that you should tell me everything, for we have more enemies than friends just now."

"Oh! I am so sorry, Paul, that I said anything to you about it. You will just worry yourself to death."

"Nay, my darling," he answered, tenderly, "if this would be my only trial, I would most gladly submit to it, but I, I—"

Here she finished the sentence, saying:

"Why, you are so superstitious."

"No, I am not that, but even if I were I have had no reason for such gloomy indulgence; but if you knew the world and its people like I do, you too would be restless and uneasy."

They were silent for a few moments, when Paul spoke:

"You won't tell me what Gerald said to you, Amy?"

"Oh! yes, I will, if you insist upon it."

"Then I do insist upon it," he answered.

"Very well. When he asked me to be his wife, and I told him I could not and would not, he said, desperately, that I should, and that he had the means in his own hands, and cost what it would, that I should be his wife."

"Then it shall cost him his life," said Paul, rising to his feet, and trembling with emotion.

A faintness seemed to come over me as I heard these words, but I still had not the power to move.

"Oh! Paul, Paul," said the girl, "do sit down and don't get so angry, it cannot injure us no matter what he says."

"Amy," he said, taking his place by her side, and resuming his tender tone, "as dearly as I love you, I would rather see you sleeping quietly beneath the flowers than to know that you would ever be the wife of such a man as Gerald Gordon."

They were here interrupted by Lord Leigh, who came in, saying that he and Lillian had been hunting them high and low.

"Don't you know your are to be our vis-a-vis for the next set?"

They answered him, both assuming very gay tones, and the three descended to the dancing-rooms together.

When I was again alone, I felt as if every object was swimming around, and I had not gained entire command over myself, when a second couple entered the harp room. What was my surprise, and displeasure too this time, when I recognized Capt. Wayland and Eleanor. They took their seats on the sofa that the two young people had just vacated.

This wily, artful woman, and this world-hardened man. I was as unable, as I was before, to move or say anything, or I would not have listened to their conversation, for I felt that it was not right, and in my inmost soul knew that it boded no good, but the nightmare that possessed me would not let me leave, or make them conscious of my presence.

Eleanor opened the conversation, by saying:

"This affair has, for a long time, engaged my attention and interest. It is needless for me to say to you how very dear your daughter is to me. She is so very charming and agreeable, I am quite sure my son would never survive the loss of her, and there are none who would so well grace the House of Gordon as your beautiful child, and I wish most truly that this marriage be consummated as soon as possible."

"The honor which you confer upon me, my lady, is so exalted, that I have not the words to express my gratitude, and I assure you your wish shall be gratified as early as practicable. Of course, I shall leave nothing undone, and my highest wish shall be realized when I shall see my daughter placed under the noble patronage of the honored and loved Countess of Gordon."

"You are most lavish in your compliments, sir, but we will adjourn to the rooms below, now that this affair is so agreeably and satisfactorily arranged, and I will see my son, and in the course of the evening will let you know what will be the most suitable time for its fulfillment."

As these last words were spoken, they made their exit. I once more breathed freely, and was rising from my seat and about to take my departure, when I was preceded by a person who had been seated, like myself, concealed from view in the opposite window, and who, to my astonishment and chagrin, I recognized as Godfrey Laughton.

CHAPTER XXIII.

TROUBLE FOR PAUL AND AMY.

THE next morning I awoke from a feverish and unquiet sleep, my dreams had been so frightful that I preferred getting up early, though no one in the house was yet astir. Being fatigued from the last night's dissipation, I threw open my shutter and greeted the first carol of the early birds, and the cool morning breezes which fanned my burning brow. As I said, my dreams the night before had been very frightful, and they, together with the two conversations I had heard, left me in a state of nervous excitement. But after I had said my prayers, and refreshed myself by a cool bath, I felt much more composed, and was able to take my book and my accustomed place near the window, and to read until the sun had kissed the dew drops from the flowers, and my little repeater on the mantle told me it was the hour of eleven. Then all were awake at the Lodge, but I did not leave my room, for the view from my window was so beautiful that I could sit for hours and look at it. Presently there came a tap at my door, and I bade the visitor enter. I was not surprised when the door opened to see that it was Paul, for there was scarcely a morning that he did not come to greet me, and to ask me how I was. But I was surprised when I looked up into his face to see a frown upon his brow, and white lines about his mouth which denoted great pain. His step was as firm and as steady, and there was no tremor in his voice and his hand as he handed me an open note, and asked me to read it; he then drew a chair near the window, and leaning his head upon his hand, looked wearily out upon the moorland. I took the note, which had been written by a trembling, nervous hand, and read the following disconnected lines:

"Oh! Paul, Paul, it seems as if God's mercy is estranged from me this morning. How am I tell you what happened last night whilst we were plighting anew our vows. You seemed to have seen in the future what I could not.. Come to me, if you can, after breakfast, and I will tell you all; but one little word to you, my noble Paul, I am your 'dauntless Amy' yet, and shall be true to the last."

"The poor child, the poor child," I thought, "what can I do for her. God help them both."

"Never mind, my boy," I said, as I drew my chair closer to him, and laid my hand upon his shoulder. "Never mind, it may not all be as bad as you think it is."

"Do you know what it is?" he said, turning towards me, with burning cheeks, and flashing eye.

"Yes, I know what it is all about."

"And then you tell me not to mind."

It was the first irritable word he ever spoke to me. He rose from his seat, and with that same determined step, and that same firm look I had noticed in the library on that November evening when he spoke of Amy and Gerald, and paced the room several times, and then left it, shutting the door violently behind him, and walked across the passage to his own chamber. I sat for a few moments only after he had left me. I was not a man to idle away time in thinking; I was soon up and doing. I crossed over to his room, and told him in a very determined manner that he must go right away to Amy's, see Capt. Wayland; and remind him of the promise he had made him some weeks before, and see Amy too, and try in some way to arrange matters so that they would be less disagreeable. This was his intention anyway; or, otherwise, in his present mood, he might have been a little rebellious. He took up his hat without saying a word, and we walked out together. I told him to meet me at the beach, that I would await him there, then bade God bless him, and watched his retreating figure out of sight.

When I reached the beach, I walked hastily up and down, feeling tired enough of life now, and trying to rack my brain for some expedient by which I could free these two young beings, who were so dear to my heart, from their oppression. To have spoken to Eleanor would have been a little less than lunacy; she was doing her work, and I saw that she was determined to do it well; and old Wayland—I knew the man too well—would have sacrificed the heart of his poor young birdling to have seen her mistress of the rich lands of Gordon. What was it to him her paling cheeks and tearful eye? the title would mend all that. "Ah! this tyrannical father, this brutal husband!" I sighed wearily, as I thought of the little use of appealing to him. Poor Amy! poor Paul! I wished that this murmuring sea would bear us away on its bosom to some unknown land, where we would be at rest. I turned from the great heaving waters to meet the poor boy as I espied him coming towards me. I saw disappointment and grief depicted in every lineament of his face.

"Well, Paul, what was your success?"

"All gloomy enough, uncle," he answered drearily. "I would not mind myself so much; but poor Amy!"

At this he broke down completely and threw himself in desperation upon the sand, looking gloomily over the unbroken waters.

"Amy," he continued, after a pause, "told me that her father vowed that these nuptials shall take place in the chapel at Gordon on the 21st of this month—ten days from to-day."

"We shall see," I heard him say under his breath.

He then spoke aloud:

"I made every effort in my power to see Captain Wayland, but he took good care to keep out of my way, sending me word that it was not worth while to talk the matter over; that he was determined; his mind was irrevocably made up, and it would only be a disagreeable interview."

I saw the boy clench his hands so tightly here that the nails penetrated the flesh, and I felt very safe at that moment in not being Captain Wayland. He presently rose to his feet, and we took our way back to the Lodge in silence. I felt that we would have to weather this storm, and I prayed inwardly that, with a Christian resignation, my boy would bear the wrongs he would have to endure. "God tempers the wind to the shorn lamb," was the only remark I ventured to make as we entered the Lodge. He made me no answer, and the bell just then sounded for breakfast.

Lord Gordon's ill health prevented him as a general thing from breakfasting with us, but on this particular morning he took his seat at the foot of the table. A dead silence fell upon all, which none seemed inclined to break, when Paul, questioned by a servant what he would have, said, shortly, "nothing;" but a fragrant cup of coffee being placed beside his plate, he hastily drank it off, excused himself, and left the room.

I saw Lord Gordon look after his retreating figure, then at Eleanor and Gerald, and then at me, and as his glance was not returned, we finished our breakfast in silence.

I sat toying with my spoon, balancing it upon the edge of my cup, whilst my thoughts were busy upon other things. I resolved to go and see Geraldine, to try if anything could be done. So, after we rose from the table, I walked hurriedly to the cottage. When I knocked at the cottage door, it was opened to me by old Nellie. Marks of recent weeping had swollen her kind old eyes, and my own voice was husky when I asked for her mistress, at seeing the old woman there, with her sympathizing face. She led me to her mistress' room in silence. There, lying on a cottage bed, was the fond, doting mother, pale and tearless, speaking words of comfort to her only child. Indeed it pleased me much to see the little Amy bearing all this with true patience, though she was as pale as a lily, and her mouth and her lips were compressed; but there was spirit in her eyes, and I knew that it was no weak character they had to deal with; only once during that visit did I see a look come into her face which was so weary and so sad that it melted my very heart to tears.

"Can nothing be done, John?" asked Geraldine of me presently.

I shook my head.

"Then Heaven help us! And Amy, my poor wounded bird, not even your mother's arms can protect you from all this."

"Never mind me," the girl answered slowly. "Never mind," she repeated, and her eyes flashed with the old fire I saw in them at first.

I leaned over and asked Geraldine if nothing would move Captain Wayland.

"No, no. I do not suppose anything will. He thinks everything is to be gained, while I know everything is to be lost," she said with a shudder.

"I wonder if he will see me?"

"I fear not. He positively refused to see Paul, and I suppose you will fare no better."

"Then I will compel him," was my answer.

But I was not so good as my word, for the man evaded me as a fish does a hook for the next week, nor did I see him until the ten days had elapsed. And now, as I think over it, it might have been so much better that I did not, for heaven only knows what might have been the consequence, as my indignation and contempt knew no bounds; and when I felt how that poor tender flower was treated, torn by so rude a hand, which should have shielded it from every blast, my excitement was beyond control.

CHAPTER XXIV.

THE QUARREL.

IT is useless to record the events of the next seven or eight days. Suffice it to say that they were fraught with much anxiety and care, and we had not advanced one iota in arranging matters satisfactorily. Gerald's engagement was publicly announced, and great preparations were going on at the Lodge in regard to it. Neither Paul nor Gerald had spoken a word to each other during those gloomy days, nor had a word escaped the lips of either about the coming event.

It was on the evening of the eighth day a little scene was enacted, which I write here, for it was a great evidence in the chain of events that followed.

I had risen early and sought Paul in his chamber. He was sitting by one of his windows in his dressing-gown, and I knew by the haggard expression on his face and the dimness of his eyes that sleep had failed to visit him the night before. I sat by and tried to console him and make him think that it was all for the best that he should be so stricken. He shrugged his shoulders a little annoyed, saying:

"Do you suppose I am going to let this thing go on without making some resistance?"

I thought the boy's mind was wandering a little, and tried to turn the conversation into a different channel; but I still noticed that old determined look in his face, and I felt that there was something that he was keeping even from me for the first time in his life. I sat with him most of the morning, and he thanked me again and again with his fine eyes for the interest I took in him, but I dared not again return to my first subject, for I knew it was the man that sat by me now and not the boy of former years—one who had a strong hand and a stronger will—and I saw that he would try to make himself master of his position.

About noon, though it was very warm, the two young men went out separately, and when dinner was announced I dined alone, for neither of them had returned. I went to my room soon after and threw myself upon my couch, wearied in body and mind. I do not suppose I had been there long when Paul returned. He came to his room, and I was about to seek him, when he was summoned to his dinner. I suppose it was about ten or fifteen minutes after that when Gerald also entered and in like manner was summoned to the dining-room. I do not know how long it was after this, but think I had taken a little nap, when I heard loud and angry voices from below. I rushed down stairs with all possible speed and entered the dining-room. There before me stood the two young men. Paul was clasping one of Gerald's hands, in which was a loaded revolver, while with the other he was holding back old Patrick, who, with tears in his eyes, was trying to part them. They were both crimsoned with rage and excitement and speaking very angrily. I went up and took the loaded pistol out of Gerald's hand and parted them, asking, in the name of heaven, what was the matter? I tried to pacify them, but no sooner had I taken my

18*

hands off than Gerald rushed again at his opponent, but was anticipated, and almost before I knew it Paul had felled him to the floor. I then begged them, for mercy sake, to desist, and laid my strong arm upon that of my adopted son. He looked at me and said: "I am sorry for your sake," and then left the room.

I went to Gerald to assist him to rise, but he told me to go away and let him alone; that he would lie there forever before I should touch him.

I sat on one of the chairs near the table, heart-sore and weary of life. I buried my face in my hands and thought of the frightful object which Geraldine had said was looming up in the future and which seemed now to be near us, crushing us with its weight of misery and care. When I raised my head from my hands, I saw that poor old Patrick was watching me, apparently as much grieved as myself.

"Poor masther!" he said, "I am so sorry about all this."

I asked him to tell me what the quarrel was about.

He said that he did not know exactly, but he thought it was about a note; that when he heard the angry voices he came in and saw Paul arrest Gerald's hand, in which was the revolver. "This is all I know," wound up the old man, "but Manning was in the room when it happened; perhaps he can tell you something."

A shudder passed through my frame here, for of all the servants at the Lodge, I disliked this one most. He was avaricious, selfish, and cunning.

I went up to Paul's room to learn from him the cause of the disturbance, but he had gone away, and I did not know for many months afterwards the real cause.

I noticed Paul left the Lodge every evening about dark and would not return until late. I could see that he was very unhappy, and hoped that these night strolls would soften his misery.

This night, as usual, he returned late, perhaps later than he was accustomed to. He came to my door and rapped gently, and I told him to come in. He merely put in his head, saying:

"Are you in bed? Then I will not disturb you. Good night."'

"Good night, my son. God bless you."

And he walked to his room.

CHAPTER XXV.

THE DEATH OF GERALD.

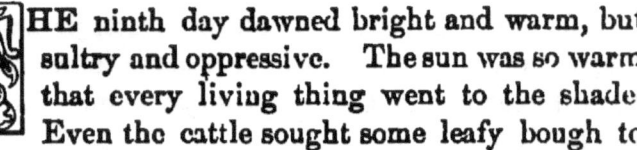HE ninth day dawned bright and warm, but sultry and oppressive. The sun was so warm that every living thing went to the shade. Even the cattle sought some leafy bough to shelter them from the burning rays. It seemed too warm for the bees to gather honey from the flowers; even if they had attempted it they would have been disappointed, for the leaves were withering and closing beneath the August sun. 'Twas the 20th of the month, and to-morrow—oh! would that to-morrow would never come!

Our breakfast was eaten in as perfect silence this morning as on the morning after the ball. Some time after we had finished, Gerald met his mother in the hall, saying:

"Mamma, I'm going to B—— this morning. I have been intending going for some time, and think this is just as good as any. I want to see some old friends there anyhow, and you know if I do not go to-day I will not have another chance."

"But, my darling, you will burn up if you attempt it. For pity sake, do not go."

"Oh! yes, I must. You know I am not sugar; there is no danger of my melting."

"But I do not want you to go, my son," persisted the mother. "I want you with me to-day. Do not go, my dearest," she entreated. "I will feel so anxious if you go away from me. And, besides, I will see so little of you in the next few months. You will go then, my son?" she continued, as she saw him buckling on his spurs.

"Yes, I will, mamma. You speak as if you were going to lose me altogether. I am sure I will be as much with you after I am married as I am now. Besides, I *must* go."

"I am very, very sorry to see you so determined, my boy. I would much rather you would not leave me. I do not feel very well, and if you go it will only make me worse."

"I do not see what my going has to do with your health, mamma. I dare say you will feel better presently."

"And will nothing keep you, my dear son?" she asked once more, so earnestly that I really felt for her.

"Nothing," was the short answer, and shortly after this, I saw him mount his horse, and his mother went up to him, saying, for the last time:

"Do not go, my son."

"Oh! yes, I must, mamma."

"Then kiss me again, darling, and take care of yourself."

She walked into the cool passage and took a seat on one of the sofas, and, for the first time in my life, I heard her sigh wearily.

All that part of the morning I saw little of Paul. When I did meet him he was silent and seemed not to care to speak to me. And indeed I thought it was for the best that we should have no more conversations just then, for, God knows, I could do no good in renewing the subject. After luncheon he left the Lodge, and I sat alone in the library as the evening wore on, and watched the heavy clouds as they gathered thick and fast in the west, betokening a storm.

I saw Eleanor from time to time looking anxiously at the road that wound around the moorland and then at the gloomy aspect of the sky, and turning to me once, she asked:

"Do you think Gerald has had time to be back, John?"

"It depends upon the swiftness of his steed and the business he was on. But, in any case, he has hardly had time to be back yet, Eleanor."

She gave another glance at the dreary road, and turning away with a sigh quite as heavy as the one she had heaved in the morning, walked to her room.

Somewhere between six and seven I went up to my own room. Black and lowering clouds were spread over the sky and not a speck of blue was anywhere to be seen. Now and then the distant rumbling of thunder was heard, seeming to awake the calmness of the sea, which was rapidly becoming troubled, lashing up its foam, as it groaned and heaved beneath the gathering tempest. And as my little repeater rang out the hour of seven it was quite dark in my room.

I sat by my window, which was still open, watching the fearful but magnificent sight, and listening to the artillery of heaven as it rolled across the vast body of water in one continuous roar. After a while the vivid lightning came flash after flash and, like an angry serpent, darting hither and thither over the murky sky. This was soon followed by the pelting rain, dashing with such fury that it robbed the flowers of their delicate petals, and beat to the earth the leaves of the great trees; dashing with such fury against my window panes that I expected every moment they would be shivered to pieces. I had never seen a more fearful tempest, and if my thoughts had not been in unison I should have shrunk from its fury; but there I sat looking over the dreary moorland, and as the lightning changed its form and came in great sheets would look vast and gloomy. There was the grove of firs, which I would catch sight of every now and then, looking more dismal than ever. My room was as black as midnight. I suppose the terrified servants had forgotten to bring me lights, and, indeed, I do not think I would have allowed them if they had come, for I enjoyed the solemnity of the scene, and the distant lashing and groaning of the sea, in concert with the booming thunder, accorded too well with my frame of mind to wish to have it disturbed. Though the storm had somewhat abated it was fearful enough still, and a heart less brave than mine would have shut out as much of its horrors as possible. Old Patrick came in during the course of it, and said:

"I see that Andrew has forgotten to bring you lights, masther; shall I bring them?"

I answered "Yes," without turning my gaze from the window, and scarcely had the word escaped my lips, when there came a flash so vivid that it almost blinded me, followed by a crash so frightful that it shook the very house to its foundation. I started to my feet, whilst the old man blest himself, saying: "The Lord be praised! what a fearful night! Holy St. Patrick pray for us!" He then went to bring the lights, whilst I moved my chair from the window and thought of the awful crash, and felt as well as I could tell that the grove of firs must have been struck. When Patrick came back with the lights, I noticed that his face was as pale as a corpse, and I asked him "What was the matter?"

"The good Lord only knows," he answered, "what it is, but I feel as if I would give my life if this night was only over."

I looked at him again, and saw that there was too much truth in his remark, and my own heart beat high, for I was not free, either, from some forebodings. He then went around and arranged everything in my room for my comfort, placing a chair here and one there, and putting down the curtains to shut out from me the dreadful tempest. After he had finished his task he retired. Some time after he left, I arose and looked at my repeater, and took out my watch and set it with the little clock, which was twenty-five minutes after eleven. I was making preparations to retire, when I was interrupted by a tap at the door, and, before I had time to speak, Eleanor entered. She had a shawl thrown around her and a night lamp in her hand.

If old Patrick had startled me a little before by his pale face, poor Eleanor startled me twice as much now.

She looked for the first time old and haggard; the lines around her mouth and deep circles around her eyes made her appear as if she had lived an age in the last few hours.

"John, what can be keeping Gerald?" she inquired, seating herself at the foot of my bed, and though it was August, she drew her heavy shawl closely around her. "I don't know what to do, I feel almost frantic. Don't you think I had better send for him? As for Lord Gordon, he won't give any advice, and says Gerald has been out many a night much later than this, and he thinks he is safe somewhere. What must I do, John?"

"Well, Eleanor, I hope, as Lord Gordon does, that he is safely housed somewhere. You know if he had left B— before the storm he would have been here long ago, and I don't think he would have ventured out in such a terrible tempest."

"But, then," she continued, "he said positively that he would come back to-night, and you know he will keep his word. I am so very, very uneasy; oh! I wish he hadn't gone. Ah! my child," speaking to the absent one, "why did you not take your mother's advice for once and stay at home? I wonder where you are now, my dearest." She buried her face in her hands and rocked herself to and fro.

"Don't make yourself so uneasy, Eleanor, I beg; go to bed and try to sleep."

"Oh! I couldn't sleep for my life; would that my boy were only here."

"You will make yourself ill, Eleanor; do try and

rest," and I passed my hand over her forehead as she leaned her head wearily against the post of the bed.

She rose presently and went to the window, drew back the curtain, and looked out upon the night. I saw her shudder, and I went and put my arm around her and took her away. I closed the curtains together again, and begged her once more to try to compose herself.

She took her lamp and walked to the door, and turning to me again, said:

"John, must I send for him?"

"Yes, do, Eleanor, if it will ease your mind at all, and, if you wish it, I will go myself."

She paused and hesitated, and then said: "Perhaps I am uselessly annoying myself; but at any rate, I don't wish you to go."

After she had left the room, I looked once more at my repeater and found it was a quarter to twelve. I then went to bed, and had scarcely done so when I heard Paul come in and soon after enter his own apartment. I closed my eyes and slept, but for how long I do not know, when my door was suddenly burst open and Patrick shook me violently, nervously saying, "for God's sake, get up, masther." I sprang from my bed, not knowing what was the matter. I hurried on my clothes with all possible haste, whilst Patrick left my room and went across to Paul's. I heard the boy exclaim, as he touched the floor, "Great heavens!" I heard many footsteps below passing up and down, and loud and soft voices, and then one shriek, which was so painful that it made my very blood curdle. I ran down stairs, taking two or three steps at a time, and soon reached the passage.

When oh! my God! what a sight met my view. The hall was crowded with men, servants and strangers, collected around one spot where some one was lying. I pushed my way through the dense crowd, and there on a bier, with his head of soft, light hair and his blue eyes glassy and dim, lay Gerald, the heir of Gordon, cold and lifeless in death. A woman's arms were clasped around him in an unconscious embrace, and that woman was poor Eleanor. I motioned one of the men to assist me, and we raised her gently and carried her to her room. I sent quickly for the family physician and then went back to the corpse. A feeling of faintness came over me, so that I staggered and fell into a chair near that bloody bier, to watch during the rest of the night. There, too, sat the stricken father at his son's head, gazing in mute agony on that pale and rigid face, his own rivaling it in whiteness, whilst every now and then a convulsive sob shook his frame. His agony was so great that my heart was wrung in pity. Paul was standing at the foot of the bier, gazing, also, on that form that had walked beside him in boyhood and manhood—the form, of all others, that had cost him most pain; all of which, I knew, was forgotten now, as I saw his clasped hands, and his heaving chest, and the look of grief and sorrow depicted in every lineament of his face.

"Where did you find him?" I asked of Michael Deasy, Lady Grantley's gardener.

"Under the grove of firs in the east end of the moorland."

I leaned over and put my hand on the heart to see if there was any sign of life there; but no! no! it was still as the grave which would soon claim it as its own. His watch, portmonie and diamond ring, and everything of value was still on his person, showing that the assassin's hand that had cut him down did not do it for pecuniary motives. The body could not be removed until the coroner's inquest was held; and oh! how those dreary hours dragged on, until the coming dawn, whilst I sat stroking from time to time the damp curls from the death-dewed boyish brow, and thinking how little should we set our hearts on anything earthly that must perish and die. Can I ever forget that fearful night? Ah! no, indeed! it is indelibly impressed upon my memory, and I seem, even now, to hear the sobs and shrieks of that poor stricken mother, calling upon her child to come back to her, "that he was not dead," "it could not be." "Ah! no, my beautiful boy, with all your fair promises of youth, health and strength you have not gone from me, my son, you will come back to your mother's heart." She would then relapse into a painful silence only to be broken by fresh bursts of sorrow. Calling upon God to restore her her child, and telling Him He was not merciful in taking him from her. "What is all this world to me if I have him not?" Then raising herself on one arm, and looking at me with a face so corpse-like that I shuddered, she said:

"John Meredith, who killed my child?"

I shook my head, for I could not answer; but she answered for me.

"I know who did it, and I will avenge you, my murdered love, my poor lost darling. May I never rest in ease either in soul or body until I see the one who did this cruel deed brought to justice."

"Do be quiet, Eleanor," I said, laying my hand upon her arm, "you are wild with grief and excitement; try and compose yourself, and God will comfort you."

"Yes, God!" she answered, frantically; "it looks as if He would comfort me who has robbed me of every earthly comfort and broken my heart."

I felt that consolation here would have as little effect as the soft rains of heaven on the solid rock. Paul tried several times during the remainder of that night and the next day to approach her to offer sympathy, but was each time rudely repulsed. At this I did not feel very much surprised, for I knew that she had never loved him, and she could not have forgotten yet the animosity that the boys bore to each other lately. Lord Gordon had not uttered a word since his son's murder had been made known to him. This was truly a blow to him, for, like Eleanor, Gerald was his only hope, and he felt all a father's love for the lifeless form beside him. The authorities had not yet arrived. I left Eleanor's room to take another look at that face in death, which in life had claimed more of my pity than my love; and as I gazed upon it so pale and cold, from which the soul had fled, I felt the tears melting in my eyes and chasing each other down my cheeks. I could scarcely believe that death had settled there, but as I touched the marble forehead with my hand, and felt once more for the pulse that had throbbed so warm and strong only a few hours before and which was now stilled, I knew but too well that the reaper had cut down this delicate plant in its early springtime. I leaned over and kissed the ice cold lips, saying: "Peace be with thee, poor child." As I did so, I heard a stifled moan from a bowed head near me, and turning, saw Paul with tears trickling through his trembling fingers.

CHAPTER XXVI.

PAUL'S ARREST.

THE officers came early in the morning, and the verdict rendered was "death by assassination." The body was then dressed for interment and laid out in the front drawing-room, the freshest and loveliest flowers having been brought to deck it. The whole affair created the most intense excitement, and many came to offer consolation to the bereaved family. We did not let Eleanor know when the body was to be removed, for the doctor was already uneasy for fear her mind would be injured by this terrible ordeal. So, noiselessly and silently we bore it away to its narrow home, and I lingered after the crowd had given way and knelt upon the tomb that contained all that was left of that mother's bright dream and a father's proudest ambition—there in his narrow cell, with the sea singing his requiem. After I arose from my knees, I found that another form had been kneeling and that I was not alone, and I felt proud of my boy to see how deeply grieved he was at the untimely end of his young relative and how entirely forgetful of how, if he had lived, he would have crossed his path and marred all his earthly happiness.

Eleanor lay in a perfect stupor for the next day or two. She asked me once "if the murderer was found." I answered "no," and she closed her eyes once more. Everyone who has witnessed death in a household knows what gloom and stillness follow; but in this house it was like the grave; the servants walked about like spirits from the unseen land, the fowls ceased their cackle in the yard, and the dogs went to sleep in the shade and were noiseless; even the birds warbled no more and deserted the branches of the trees near the Lodge. I sat most of the time in poor Eleanor's room, whom, from my very heart, I pitied, and all her faults were forgotten as I looked at that face so old now in its utter desolation. "God comfort her," I would murmur, "and pour balm into her wounded heart."

It was on the evening of the second day after poor Gerald was laid to rest that I left her perhaps a little easy and more quiet and went up to Paul. He was lying on the bed with his face downward buried in the pillow. I touched him on the shoulder, and when he raised his face I stepped backwards in astonishment at seeing it so pale and haggard. I told him to get up, that he should walk, that he was making himself sick. He rose without seeming to have any will of his own, and took his gloves off of the dressing-table. I followed him down stairs, and, seeing my hat, took it and walked out with him. I suppose it was about four o'clock when we went forth. We walked on rapidly for awhile and then slackened our pace, all the while in silence. I had not observed where we were going until we had neared the sea, which was as deadly calm as the Lodge, after the storm which had disturbed it two or three nights before. I don't remember much about what happened this evening, how long we were out, or what we spoke about when we did speak, only I know that when we were about returning I noticed two men approach us riding rapidly. As they came near I saw they were officers. I was very much surprised when they jumped from their horses as they came up to us. Both bowed to me very respectfully and said something about "*unpleasant*" and "*compelled*." Then one of them, laying his hand upon Paul's shoulder, said:

"John Paul Stewart, I arrest you in the Queen's name for the murder of Gerald, heir of Gordon."

"My God!" was all I could say, and everything became dark; I felt as if an iron hand was clasping my throat, and I fell insensible at the men's feet.

When I returned to consciousness, there was quite a little crowd collected around me, and my old friend, Dr. Arnold, was rubbing my hand. One or two of the old servants from the Lodge were there, Patrick being one of them, and were sobbing like children, while near the prisoner stood the noble form of Lord Leigh and the light and graceful one of Anthony Gay. They were both speaking to Paul, telling him "that no matter what the verdict said, they would believe, as they did now, from their very hearts, that he was innocent." Murmurs of discontent were heard in the crowd, which was rapidly increasing, for here was the man who had extended his hand to the poor and had given charity to the widow and the orphan, who had been received into the halls of the noble and great, being one of the brightest ornaments there, and to whom none could have imputed an act unworthy of the Christian and the gentleman, stigmatized as a murderer.

"I will nae believe it! I will nae believe it!" said

an old woman, coming forward. "Nae, nae, I canna believe that this bairn, who was sa noble and gleeful, should have been guilty of sa bloody a deed. Nae, my bonny one, let them say what they please, your auld Scotch friend will nae believe them."

For the first time tears came into Paul's eyes, and the two young men beside him showed great signs of emotion.

"Never mind, Walter," he said, in return to a question from Lord Leigh, "it will be all right yet."

Before the crowd augmented they took him away, and the old doctor put me in his buggy and drove me to Geraldine's, for I could not go back to the Lodge. I found that they had just heard the dreadful news, and they were all seemingly as sad as myself.

I cannot bear to write about those dark days, they were so gloomy and so miserable, and I would that they could be blotted out from my memory forever.

CHAPTER XXVII

THE TRIAL.

FEW events occurred of any importance between the day of the arrest and the day of the trial, which took place on the 24th of the following month, except that we who loved him were very sad that he was shut up in a prison, and we felt sure of his innocence.

I remember that I was allowed to speak a few words in private to him before the witnesses were examined, but I will not give the conversation I had with him until after the trial. The court was then called to order, and we took our seats.

The first witness was the innkeeper at B—, the town that Gerald visited the evening he was murdered. I will not give the questions or cross-questions, save a few of them, but will simply give the man's evidence as he stated it. He began:

"Gerald, heir of Gordon, came to my inn the 9th of August. Most of the day he was closeted with some of his friends. At one time, in the public room, he seemed very restless and agitated. One of his comrades asked him what was the matter. He shrugged his shoulders and answered he didn't know, but he supposed a man on the eve of his marriage day was not as composed as usual, but he pitied them if they all were as badly off as he was. About half after three he came to me and said he believed he would lie down, that his head ached. I had a room instantly prepared for him, and he went directly to it. I suppose it was half an hour, or perhaps three-quarters, after that when I went myself to see if he wanted anything. I opened the door softly and saw him sitting at the window smoking a cigar, looking out upon the sky in the direction of his home. I asked him if he had slept any. 'No,' was the moody answer, and then in the same breath, 'Get my horse I want to go down to Dalton's.' (Dalton was one of the young men who had visited him that day.) In about ten or fifteen minutes after that I saw him riding at full speed in the direction of his friend's. I don't know exactly how long after this it was before he came back, but suppose it was an hour and a half or two hours. His horse was smoking and foaming with hard riding and he himself seemed to be very much fatigued. He threw himself upon two chairs in my public room and closed his eyes. I went up to him and asked him if he wouldn't lie down. He answered 'no,' and then ordered his supper, telling me to make haste, as he wanted to go home. He closed his eyes again, and I went to have supper prepared for him.

"It was now very dark, and the storm had just begun to rage without. When his supper was ready I went in myself to wait upon him. He ate very little and complained that the coffee was not good and that the waffles hadn't risen well. I made no answer, for I saw that he was out of sorts. He stayed a long time at the table after he had finished, toying with his teaspoon. Whenever I spoke to him he answered me in monosyllables or very abruptly. Hearing some one enter the public room, he asked me to go and see if it was Dalton. I went to see, and came back and told him 'no.' 'What can be keeping him?' he said, whilst an angry frown contracted his brow. 'He promised to be here at eight.' 'It is twenty minutes after eight, sir, and I don't suppose he will come in such a storm,' I ventured to remark. He rose from the table then and looked out. The lightning flashed in his face as he opened the door. 'This is enough to wake the dead,' he said, as the flash was followed by a burst of thunder. Then, turning to me, he said: 'I want my horse quickly.' 'Oh! sir,' I pleaded, 'do not go out in such a tempest. You may be killed by the lightning.' 'I want my horse,' he repeated. I had the poor animal ordered, and it was somewhat refreshed with its meal of oats and short rest. After the horse was brought around, the deceased hesitated about going. I suppose he returned twenty times after starting, sometimes to ask one question, then another, and another time made the excuse that he wanted to light his cigar, that the rain had put it out. The last time he came back he asked me to lend him an umbrella, and I went into my wife's room to get one. She was sick at the time, and she had to have an opiate every hour. She reminded me of it as I entered the room, and I looked at the clock and saw that the hands pointed to nine. I lingered in the room a few moments after she had taken it, and then went out into the public room. The deceased was sitting at a little side-table, with his head in his hands. He did not notice my entrance, and I was very quiet, and I know that it must have been at least a quarter of an hour before he roused himself.

He started up suddenly and asked for the umbrella. The storm was now at its height, and as he opened the door the rain dashed in in torrents and the thunder rocked the house like a cradle. I ventured once more to beg him not to go, but he made no answer, and in a few moments I heard him urging his horse at full speed."

"How long do you suppose it would have taken him to ride from your house to Gordon Lodge?" asked the judge.

The man replied without any hesitation:

"It is measured ten English miles. The deceased always rode the finest and most spirited horses. The one he rode this particular evening was to be sure a little jaded and the condition of the roads was not good. So, I would say, reckoning all this, it would take him *full two hours.*"

The next witness called was Michael Daisy, Lady Grantley's gardener. Thir old man in giving in his evidence would tell his own story, much to the amusement of some present:

"Well," he began. "I had gone on the 19th of August to sit at the wake of Andrew Murphy, who had died that morning of fever, at six o'clock, in company with Patrick Donahoe and Timothy Noonan. Poor Andrew—the Lord rest him—lived two miles on the north side of the grove of firs on the moorland. At eleven o'clock that night I was sitting at the wake."

"How do you know it was eleven o'clock, Michael?" asked the counsel.

"Why, the clock told me, your honor, and no one

could have told me better; and oh! if you remember, your honor, it was one of the most dreadful of nights. I never saw such lightning or heard such thunder; it was flash after flash and then such a roar as the thunder would give. But as I sat there I remembered my Lady had given me some orders about her flowers, which went out of my head entirely, and I thought what a drenching their pretty heads would get, for the rain was coming down as if the sea was turned bottom upwards, and I feared the big drops would take off their dresses altogether if I did not go to them; and then I thought of my Lady's sad face when she saw that they were spoilt. I asked Patrick Donahoe to come home with me. 'I, faith,' he answered, 'catch me making a goose of myself, as you are green enough to do. I have too much respect for my new hat and coat than to give them a ducking such a night as this.' I told Pat he was a hard case and turned to Tim Noonan, who was nodding his head in the corner in the face of the dead, and snoring away, until I thought charity compelled me to ask him to go home. 'Faith that I will,' said he, 'for I have been dreaming ugly dreams in that straight-jacket of a chair.' (And this sleep could be excused in poor Tim, who had sat up every night with the sick man.) Well, your honor, after bidding all the people good night we started home. The night was so dark and the storm so great that we could not see each other sometimes. Amid the roaring of the thunder I would ascertain if he was near me. When we got within several yards of the grove of firs, Tim said, 'Mike, dear, is this you? No,' he answered, before I had time to speak, 'it is a horse and no rider upon him. I suppose the poor fellow has been struck by the lightning.' 'Faith, it looks bad enough,' said I, 'but let us go here to the firs and shelter ourselves a while.' So in I stepped and Tim followed me. I had walked in a few steps, when I stumbled over something and fell, and felt that it was the form of a man. I called Tim, and he came to me by the sound of my voice, and I told him to feel and see what it was. He felt it, and said, 'yes, that it was a man, that the poor creature must have been killed by the lightning, and that must have been his horse we had just seen.' I had a match-box in my pocket, so I took it out and struck a light. I told Tim to hold his hat up, so the rain would not fall upon it. He did so, and I saw by the light of it a man lying with his face downwards and blood running from his head. One of the big firs had been struck by lightning, and I thought the poor fellow had been hit by one of the branches. We turned him over and saw it was the young Lord at the Lodge. One of his hands was grasping his coat near his heart; the other had a gash on it right across the fingers, like it had been cut with a knife. I felt my blood run cold as I looked at him, and it was a terrible sight, your honor. We ran back to the wake and told the men there, who came with us immediately. We made a rude kind of frame by the light of the lantern we had, and we lifted the poor thing from the ground and laid him upon it, and carried it home to his poor mother. And I pray the good Lord that I may never see such a sight again if I live to be as old as Mathusalum."

This was Michael's evidence, and he stood all the questions and cross-questions without deviating the least from it. He was then asked what time he supposed it was when he came to the grove the first time. He said he could not tell exactly, but when they went back for help to the wake it was a quarter to one, and that it was two by the big clock at the Lodge when they laid the body in the hall. As I said before, it was impossible to prevent Michael from going on in his own simple way, and as he was a very important witness there was not much objection made.

The next witness was Timothy Noonan, and as his evidence coincided with Michael's in every particular, I will not give it here.

Old Patrick was the next witness called. There were tears in his aged eyes, and his voice often choked with emotion as he gave the following evidence:

"I have been with the prisoner from his infancy to his manhood, and he was as lovely a boy and as noble a man as ever the bright rays of the sun shone upon. He was a model of honor, truth and moral worth, and was as gentle and as tender as a woman in disposition." (He here paused to brush away a tear that was trickling down his honest face.) He was then asked if the deceased and the prisoner had been on amicable terms with each other up to the time of the murder.

He answered:

"No, he did not think they lived upon exactly amicable terms, though generally they were very polite and gentlemanly towards each other."

He was then asked what he meant by saying that he

did not think they lived exactly upon amicable terms, and he said he meant "that sometimes disputes arose between them."

He was then questioned if he ever witnessed anything more serious than a dispute between them.

He answered:

"Yes, once, when they were children, and once since they were grown."

He was then commanded to tell the time the one occurred since they were grown, and I saw that the old man very reluctantly replied:

"On the 18th of August."

Patrick was then told to give all the particulars of the quarrel, and he did so in the following words:

"On the evening of the 18th, the prisoner came in some time after the dinner-hour. Both the prisoner and the deceased left the Lodge soon after breakfast that morning, separately. I went to the prisoner's room soon after he came and told him that his dinner was ready. He rose silently, and preceded me to the dining-room. Shortly after this, the deceased entered, and soon after joined the prisoner at the table. I was there when he came in, and noticed that they did not speak to each other. I remained but a few moments after that in the room—I was called away to attend to something I had neglected that morning in an adjoining room. I don't know how long I had been there when I heard very loud voices from the dining-room. I could not tell what the words were that were uttered, but I went in as speedily as possible, and found that the prisoner had arrested the arm of the deceased, in the hand of which was a loaded pistol. They were both very much excited. I was too frightened to remember what was said by either of them, but, shortly after I entered, the prisoner let the deceased's arm go. The deceased then rushed at the prisoner with the intention of striking him, but the blow was parried, and the prisoner knocked the deceased down and left the room. I did not see the prisoner again until the next evening, when he came back between eleven and twelve, or I think it was nearer to twelve, though I do not exactly remember. I, myself, opened the door for him. He was very wet from the rain, and stopped in the passage to hang his hat up."

"Did he speak to you, or did you notice any agitation in his manner?" he was asked.

"Yes," answered the old man, slowly, "but he bade me good night as usual, and left the room."

He was here questioned and cross-questioned a great deal, but he gave the same answers all the time. He was then told to go on, and he continued:

"I soon after went to my own room to prepare for bed. I don't know how long I slept, when I was wakened by the porter, who rapped very loudly at the door, telling me to rise quickly. I put on my clothes as quickly as possible, and opened the door for him. He was as white as a magnolia leaf, and trembled like an aspen. 'Something dreadful has happened,' he said, 'our young Lord has been murdered.' I trembled now in my turn, and enquired for the particulars. He said he could not give them to me, for all that he knew was the body had been found in the grove of firs. I then went to alarm the house. I found Lady Gordon in the passage, who seemed not to have slept any. I led her to her room and she seemed as tractable as a child. I never saw her so before. I then went to wake my masther and the prisoner. My masther was the first one I waked. I then went to the prisoner's room. He seemed violently agitated, and exclaimed 'My Heavens!' when he heard the dreadful tidings I brought. During the rest of the night the prisoner seemed very much grieved, and twice I saw him shed tears, and he remained near the bier the whole night, and no inducement would persuade him to leave it. Even at the grave he lingered longest, and had a look of real pain in his face."

He was here cross-questioned again, and this finished his evidence.

The next called up was Manning, the head dining-room servant at the Lodge, who was present during the quarrel between the two young men.

It is unnecessary to give all of his evidence, so I will only give the part that related to the quarrel, as the rest of it coincided with Patrick's.

He began:

"On the evening of the 18th of August, I was in the dining-room when the prisoner came in. He sat down at the table in silence, and I suppose had been there ten or fifteen minutes when the deceased entered. He, also, took his place at the table in silence, and only staid there a few minutes and did not eat much. As he rose to leave, he drew his handkerchief from his pocket, and, in doing so, a note dropped from his pocket to the floor, very near the prisoner, who picked it up and said it was his own. 'It is not yours,' said the deceased, coming up to him. 'I say it is,' answered the prisoner, 'and I wish to know how it came into your possession?' I do not remember the deceased's answer, and there was a great deal more passed between them that I do not remember. At length the deceased went to snatch the note from the prisoner's hand, who raised his arm to strike him. The deceased then drew a revolver, but the prisoner arrested it before he had time to fire."

The rest of the evidence the reader is acquainted with, and it is too painful for me to repeat it here. This witness expatiated largely on the merits of poor Gerald; for some reason of his own, making his evidence as hard on the prisoner as possible. I saw Lord Leigh frown angrily several times whilst he was speaking, and heard Anthony Gay, who was also near me, call him repeatedly a villain.

The last witness was Godfrey Laughton.

He approached the witness stand with the same ease and grace that always characterized him, and in his high-toned, cultivated voice gave in his evidence thus:

"I have known the prisoner about two years, but I cannot say that I have known him intimately. He was generally cold and stiff in his demeanor towards me, though always gentlemanly. I think, from my own personal knowledge of him and the deceased, that they were not on good terms. I overheard a conversation, on the the evening of the 10th of August, at Lady Grantly's, which convinced me of this fact. I was in Lady Grantly's harp-room, in one of the windows smoking, when the prisoner and a lady entered. I paid little attention to what they were saying until I heard the prisoner exclaim: 'If Gerald Gordon insists upon marrying Miss Wayland it will cost him his life!' Almost immediately after this they left the room."

Laughton was here asked if he did not see the lady, too. He answered positively, "No," that he was seated so that he could only see the gentleman; "nor could I have recognized the tones of her voice, for they were very low and soft."

(I had also noticed on that eventful night how softly and sweetly Amy spoke in the harp-room, and I could not help but admire and feel grateful to Laughton for his delicacy in thus preventing her being brought before the court.)

The witness continued:

"I did not see the prisoner after that until the 19th day of August. One of my tenants had died that morning, and I went down to see if I could do anything for his distressed family. On my return, as I approached the grove of firs on the moorland, I was somewhat surprised at seeing the prisoner emerge from them. He scarcely recognized me, seemed very much agitated, and walked away as rapidly as possible. I saw him again that night, somewhere about eleven. I had gone to Andrew Drew's, an old friend of mine, who lives at Mount Fair, some time before the storm commenced. The time was very pleasantly spent, and it was near ten o'clock when I arose to return home.

My friend begged me to remain with him, as it was raining very heavily. I told him an old soldier did not mind the rain. Then he insisted upon accompanying me, and all I could say or do would not dissuade him from going part of the way. The hard rain prevented us from making rapid progress, and the lightning was vivid and continuous. When we had gotten within about a quarter of a mile of the firs, I saw, by a brilliant flash of the lightning, a man standing under one of the trees, not far from the grove. My companion also saw him, and we both thought it strange that he should be there during such a violent storm. As we came up to him, I said, 'Friend, what are you doing here during such a fearful storm? If you have no way of going home, jump up here behind me and I will take you.'

"'Thank you, but don't mind me,' was the brief reply.

"When he spoke, I exclaimed, in astonishment: 'Why, Paul, are you here?' for I instantly recognized his voice. He said nothing, but another vivid flash showed him to me as plainly as I ever saw him in my life. 'You'll be drowned,' I continued, 'if you stay out here much longer: you had better come with me.' 'No, no; the roads are too heavy for any animal to carry two, and, besides, I can shorten the distance by going through the fields,' he answered. Andrew Drew then offered him his horse, as he had much further to walk than himself. This offer he also refused, telling Andrew that he was very kind and extending his hand to him. He then begged us to go on and not to tarry in the rain on his account, and that he would soon be at home himself. I here insisted upon Andrew's returning home, and I took my way to Merry Hall, leaving the prisoner where we had found him."

Andrew Drew's evidence was the same as this given here, and his ended the examination of witnesses. I don't know how to describe my feelings whilst the jury was forming the verdict. I must have been sustained by excitement, for I was wild with apprehension. At last the jury entered, and to the question—"Guilty or Not Guilty?" "*Guilty!*" was the answer, and for a while I lost consciousness. As I returned to my senses, the awful sentence of death by hanging was being pronounced upon the prisoner.

And was this all my glory and all my pride—the looming gibbet? Indeed, I was truly an old man now. Ah! never, never would I look upon this world again with its joys and its pleasures, for my heart was in the lonely cell with the lonely prisoner, and would follow him wherever he went, even to the grave.

I asked Lord Leigh what my poor boy said when asked why the sentence of death should not be pronounced against him. He answered that his appeal was short, simple and touching, and that he had taken it down in his note book, and handed it to me. I will insert it here:

"My friends, if such you will permit me to call you after having heard me, like Cain, branded as a murderer, I protest here, in the presence of my Divine Maker, that I am innocent of so dreadful a crime. Many of you weep for me, and your tears fall, as the gentle rains from heaven, soothing and refreshing, upon a withered plant which has been blighted by a rude blast. Gerald Gordon was not my enemy, and I never slew him. So far was I from murdering him, that I would now most willingly give my life to see him back in his mother's arms. I stand, as it were, alone in this great world. Few would mourn for me were I in his place. Perhaps a tear from some kind friend might fall in tribute to my memory, but when that dried all remembrances would float away as the sea winding on to the distant ocean. But for him, whom the reaper spared not in his spring time, but cut away, as the harvester does his golden grain, unmindful of the flowers, there weeps a grief-stricken mother, who wafts her heaving sighs to the 'sepulchre by the sea,' where, clasped in the arms of the still visitor, sleeps her first and only born, his fair hair covered over by the death dews. Her heart has been a fearful wreck since his young life blood ebbed and flowed and sprinkled the green turf beneath the dark grove on the moorland. There is a father, too, who has grown old since the eyes of his darling were closed forever, and he mourns for the day that will never return, when he heard those lips, now cold and bloodless and hushed in death, calling his name. Ah! again I say that I would give my life to redeem his. Oh! my friends, this is a sad ordeal. There was, truly, a sorrow that was robbing my life of its brightness and youth, and the form that rendered its soul to its Maker there," pointing to the dark grove, "was accessory to that grief. But believe me, my friends, when I say that this was not sufficient to make me a homicide. I can only pray to be resigned to my hard, hard fate, leaving the rest to that Eye that marks the sparrow's fall and which never sleeps."

In all that vast assembly there was scarce an eye but was moist by a tear, and scarcely a lip from which a sigh did not escape. And as they bore him away to his dungeon, a murmur arose which was heartrending to hear, and the lamentations were long and sad.

CHAPTER XXVIII.

A REPRIEVE GRANTED.

THE night was cold and raw, and the drizzling rain came down slow and penetrating, causing the unlucky ones who were exposed to it to shake and shiver. It fell noiselessly upon the roofs of the houses in the great city of London. My own heart was as cheerless as this dreary night as I rang the bell at the door of my old friend the duke whom I introduced to you at Gordon Lodge in the summer of 18—, when Paul was but a little boy. I had met him frequently since and had long numbered him among my warmest and most intimate friends. Nor had he forgotten the child whose curly head he had stroked on that summer's evening many years ago, and who had won his way to the old man's heart and was still tenderly cherished there. My summons was answered by a grey-headed butler, who ushered me into a warm, comfortable drawing-room, where brilliant lights formed a strange contrast to the gloom without and to the dreariness of my weary, worn heart. I had not long to wait when the door opened and the old duke entered. He grasped my hand warmly without speaking, and we seated ourselves in silence. After a pause of a few moments he spoke to me, saying:

"This is a sad meeting truly, my dear friend. You have had my deepest sympathy throughout the whole of this sad affair, and I am the more deeply grieved because I firmly believe in the innocence of this poor young man."

"Then you really believe that he is innocent after the convincing evidence you have heard?"

"I do, indeed," was the honest answer of this noble gentleman.

"Oh! I thank God there is one who believes with me."

"Not only one, but the numbers are multiplied who believe him guiltless."

"Ah!" I sighed, "when I think of him in his lonely prison, with no comforting voice, no kind word, to lighten his heavy heart, it is hard, hard to bear."

"Do not your suspicions rest upon any one?" asked the duke.

"No, I have no cause to suspect any one. I only know that my poor boy is free from this stain."

"Then we must have a reprieve to give us time to look around."

"That is my business here now, and, my dear friend, I beg that you will render me your valuable assistance."

"With all my heart! with all my heart!" was the kind reply. "I feel that I cannot do too much for this young friend of mine, and I am entirely at your service. The sentence is to be put into execution on the 25th of November, isn't it?"

"Yes."

"And this is—"

"The first of October," I answered.

"I will use all my influence, Mr. Meredith, to get you a reprieve, and one for as long a period as possible."

"Oh! yes, yes," I cried, "for as long a period as possible."

"I noticed that the gentleman speaking in the counsel for the defence was very eloquent. This young Lord Leigh has quite distinguished himself, and seems to have spoken from a heart teeming with the highest esteem and love for the prisoner."

He here abruptly asked:

"Are you personally acquainted with this Godfrey Laughton? I see that his evidence has borne great weight with the jury."

"Yes, I have known him for some time."

"Sufficiently to have formed an estimate of his character?"

"No," hesitatingly, "but I don't think I am very much prepossessed in his favor."

The duke looked into the fire musingly for a few moments, but did not pursue the subject, and shortly afterwards I arose to take my departure. The kind gentleman insisted upon my remaining and partaking of his hospitality. I thanked him warmly, but said "that I must go back to my hotel, where rooms were prepared for me." I then bade him good night and walked out, feeling easier in mind than I had yet done in those weary days of anxiety and care.

As I entered the public room of the hotel my attention was arrested by the mention of Paul's name, made by one of a group of young men, who were sitting somewhat apart from the crowd smoking. He was saying:

"I don't care what jury convicted Paul Stewart, I

don't believe he is guilty, although I know the evidence is enough to condemn St. Peter were he placed in a similar position."

"I am sure of his innocence, too," added a second, taking a cigar from his mouth and puffing the smoke into the air. "I knew Stewart at college, and he was the finest fellow there; but that Gordon, poor fellow, was as weak as a girl. I feel sorry for him now that he is dead and gone, but I never liked him much while living."

"Well, here," said a third, "is a health to Stewart, and that he may soon be out of that gloomy prison back in his old place amongst us," and he drank off a glass of champagne.

I here went to my room, thinking of the old duke's remark: "The numbers are multiplied who believe in his innocence," and I lay down much comforted in mind and slept until morning.

I staid but as short a time as I possibly could in London, but did not leave until the reprieve was granted and signed with the royal seal. I then turned my face homeward with the duke as my companion, thanking God in my inmost soul for His goodness in thus granting me a longer time to think and to act.

The locomotive whistled loud and clear on the still autumn air as we took our seats for the town of B—. The ride seemed long and wearisome to me, for I was most anxious to be at home, and I was delighted when the train at last stopped and we got off on the platform, where my carriage was in waiting. I handed in the duke, and following, took my seat beside him.

"Shall we go to the prison to-night?" he asked.

"I shall go, but I prefer that you should go to the hotel and rest and refresh yourself after your tiresome trip."

"No, no, I am not tired, and am most anxious to see my young friend."

"To the prison, driver," he called, without waiting for me to give the order.

I sat back in the carriage with my heart overflowing with gratitude to this good old man, who seemed never to weary in doing good. When we reached the prisoner's cell, we found Paul sitting by a small deal table, on which burned a solitary lamp. He was reading with his elbow resting on the table. The noise of our entrance roused him, and he came forward with both hands extended. I took him in my arms and pressed him to my heart, and noticed a smile of gratitude light up his face. And when the duke caught him by both hands and wrung them warmly, tears filled his eyes.

"My son," he said, "I pledge to you my belief in your perfect innocence, and I have come here with the express purpose of seeing you and telling you this."

"Ah! sir, you have performed an act worthy of the true Christian in coming to the captive's cell and in speaking words which are so comforting and gratifying to me. Unwilling, though the sentence has been passed, to believe me a homicide, I feel now as if I could face the dreadful gibbet with fewer pangs."

After a few moments the duke spoke:

"We hope to do a great deal for you now; a reprieve is granted you, which is of some length, and in that time we will not be idle in your service, and hope to accomplish much. So be of good cheer and all will yet be well."

"Thank you! thank you!" was all the boy could utter.

As our time was limited, we soon arose and bade him good night. He whispered to me as I was leaving:

"Tell my poor Amy to cheer up; that a golden sunbeam may yet shine for us."

I nodded, and we again entered our carriage and drove to the hotel.

CHAPTER XXIX.

MRS. WAYLAND AND HER DAUGHTER.

THE days were fast rolling on, and still no clue to the murderer. I went one evening to Geraldine's. I entered the quiet little hall and rapped gently at her chamber door. Amy opened it for me, whispering "speak softly," and instead of inviting me in, came out into the passage and closed the door noiselessly behind her. We then walked to the little green parlor, and sitting on the sofa beside me, she told me that her mother had been very sick ever since the day that Paul had been convicted.

"Dr. Arnold has told me not to be too confident of her recovery, and to keep her very quiet. And this morning papa came to me with a proposal of marriage from Godfrey Laughton, which, of course, I refused. This enraged papa, but I was firm and determined. Papa then said that I should obey him."

"I marry Godfrey Laughton!" she continued, with the old fire flashing in her eyes. "Never! never! and I told papa so."

The excitement soon ended and the soft look came back into her face as she told me "that it all resulted in making her poor mother much worse."

After I had delivered Paul's message, she asked me "if she could not go sometimes to see him?" I told her "yes; that I would consider it, and perhaps obtain her permission to do so."

"Do, do," she said, "for I must see him. But there is Godfrey Laughton," she broke off suddenly. "What must I do with him? Oh! don't leave me, uncle," catching me by the sleeve and holding me beside her on the sofa.

He entered in the same bland manner that was usual with him, offering each of us his hand in turn. As I did not give way to him, he made his visit very short. When he was about leaving, he asked Amy if he might call the following evening and see her alone?

"Mr. Laughton," she answered, coldly, "there is no time I can call my own since my mother's illness. My mornings and my evenings are employed in attendance on her."

"I am sorry to hear this, but yet do not despair of seeing you," and, bowing gracefully, he left us.

We did not speak after he was gone, but watched his retreating figure.

"My mistress wishes to see Mr. Meredith," said old Nellie, putting her head in at the door.

"Go and comfort her, and try to make her troubled mind easier," whispered Amy at her mother's room, whilst she passed out into the autumn sunshine to refresh her drooping spirits.

Geraldine held out her wasted hand to me as I entered her chamber.

"I am so glad you have come, John. I have wanted to see you for a long time."

I sat down by her bedside and looked upon that gentle face of which I was so fond. The blue veins were distinct and clear now upon the white forehead, there were large circles under the pale blue eyes, and bright feverish spots burned upon each cheek. I passed my hand over the smooth, warm forehead, and asked if she felt better.

"No, I will never feel better again here, John, and the next autumn leaves will fall upon my narrow bed, for I will not linger much longer in this valley of tears. You have been a kind, good friend to me, and my happiness for many years has proceeded from your friendship. I will leave this world with but little regret, my only one being that my poor child will be left behind, and I would wish to live to see Paul's innocence declared, for I know it must be some day, and you will live to see it. There is one thing, John, I want to beg you to promise me, and it is after I am gone, not to let my poor Amy marry Godfrey Laughton. Will you stand by her, and shelter and protect her?" She leaned upon her elbow and looked steadily into my eyes.

"I will," I answered firmly.

"Then God be blessed! for now I will die happily."

Here were two children bequeathed to me by their dying mothers, and I felt that my responsibility was growing heavy and heavier as I sat still gazing upon that gentle face, with its closed eyes and sharp, marked outlines, and knew that a martyr's crown would soon rest upon those soft tresses in a better land.

In the evening when I left her I walked down towards the sea. When I came within a short distance of the grove of firs, I saw a man examining the ground very near it, almost in it, evidently in search of something. He saw me coming, and walked rapidly away, but I was not mistaken in that graceful carriage, and wondered what Godfrey Laughton was looking for there.

CHAPTER XXX.

JOHN LOSES A RELATIVE.

SEVEN months had passed in quick succession, carrying with them the autumn frosts and the winter snows; and, as I stood on the piazza at Gordon, a great bee buzzed by me, giving the cheery announcement that spring had come; while out on the lawn, swarms of small flies were commencing to take wing and light upon the nearest bud or flower. The jonquills, hyacinths, violets, and Easter flowers were all in bloom, and scenting the air with their fragrant breath; the lawn looked like a smooth green carpet, ornamented here and there by a glistening dew-drop, the birds were twittering and carolling, and all nature seemed alive with joy.

Eleanor and Lord Gordon had not been at the Lodge for many months. When Eleanor was able to travel, they had taken her away to Italian skies, to bring the roses back to her cheeks; they had not yet returned, and in all probability would not during the summer. There was still no clue to the murderer, and the reprieve would expire in June. The Duke had written to me that he thought he could have it extended if necessary, but still I was very miserable, thinking of poor Paul wasting his young life away in a gloomy prison. The air was so balmy and soft this spring morning, that I took my chair out on the balcony. I had not been there very long, when I saw Geraldine's servant, old Nellie, approaching me. I knew she wanted me, so I advanced to meet her.

"Well, Nellie, what news this morning?"

"Bad enough, bad enough, Mr. Meredith. Come right away to my poor mistress, she has but a few hours to live; and that darling child, Amy, is breaking her heart, come, come."

We hastened with all possible speed to the cottage, and as I went into the sick room, I saw that a great change had taken place in the invalid. Her face had sunken, and the dews of death were fast gathering on her brow. She recognized me as I walked to her bed, and a faint smile played over her features for an instant. Amy was holding her hand in hers, counting the feeble, flickering pulse, and in every lineament of her young face was depicted despair. I leaned over the dying mother, and heard her praying softly, invoking blessings upon her child, with whose name she coupled mine and Paul's. She would then make an appeal for her erring husband, calling upon God to be merciful to him, and bring him to Himself, and then relapse into asking blessings for Amy.

I lifted the disengaged hand which lay upon the coverlid, and felt that the pulse was growing fainter and slower, and rapidly ebbing away. I could hardly feel sorry that she was going, for her life had been so full of anguish and of care, and now her spirit would soon be peaceful and at rest by her Heavenly Father's side; but for Amy, my heart bled, as she sat motionless, not daring to speak for fear she would snap the cord that bound her loved mother to earth. Geraldine spoke:

"Amy, my darling, are you near me?"

"Yes, mother, do you want anything?"

"Nothing, dearest, only to die in your arms."

I placed her head upon the breast of her daughter, who lovingly twined her arms around her. I don't know where Captain Wayland was; old Nellie had sought for him, but he could not be found. I was very anxious that he should come in time, hoping that when he saw his gentle wife leaving him forever, that his hard heart might be touched at last. I knew that I would miss very much her soft smiles, her enduring, patient look, and her poor, pale face, and I sighed to think what a blank she would leave in my life.

The day passed on, but we did not relinquish our seats; everything was still and quiet in that death-chamber. The breath of the flowers stole softly in at the open windows, whilst notes from the forest warblers struck upon our ears in sweet and musical tones. And the little clock on the mantle ticked away its seconds, its minutes, and its hours. Slower and slower beat that heart which was bowed down with its weight of care, fainter and fainter throbbed the pulse, and shorter and shorter grew the breath, and with a smile that was sweet and heavenly, the spirit took its flight.

I removed her from the arms of her child, and closed the blue eyes, clasped the slender fingers over the breast, smoothed the fair hair on the marble brow, and kissed, for the last time, her cold lips. There was a low cry near me, and I turned and remembered that there was an afflicted heart that I must comfort. I bore Amy from the room where lay all that remained of her truest and best friend, who would soon be consigned to the lap of earth. I rubbed Amy's temples with cologne water, as she lay pale and still. I then left her and walked from room to room in that little cottage, where I had seen the poor mother's patient face, and heard her kind voice so often in the last twelve years. We buried her the following evening in the quiet graveyard on a little knoll that looked towards the sea.

The southern sun kissed the green mound as it rose from the calm waters, and the gentle dews sprinkled the turf, and called into life the violets and the roses. Not long after, a little white tombstone rose in that churchyard, simply bearing her name, and around which the myrtle and the ivy twined caressingly.

"*Requiescat in pace,*" I murmured, as I cast a fond look at her last resting-place, and left the spot.

CHAPTER XXXI.

THE OIL PAINTING.

FELT lonely enough at Gordon Lodge by myself, old Patrick being my only companion, and now that poor Geraldine was no more, there was little for me to think about but my trials, and how to prove Paul's innocence. Amy was more resigned, and her father much kinder, not urging her any more to her marriage with Godfrey, nor had he mentioned it since his wife's death.

I was feeling so lonely and wretched one evening that I determined to walk back to the cottage, though I had been there in the morning. It was rather late when I left the Lodge, and the moon was peeping up from the sea as I neared the cottage. As I opened the white gate and entered, Amy's sweet voice fell upon my ear, singing a ballad from Longfellow; she had reached the second verse, and I heard:

> "My life is cold, and dark, and dreary,
> It rains, and the wind is never weary,
> My thoughts still cling to the mouldering past,
> And the hopes of my youth fall thick in the blast,
> For the day is dark and dreary."

"Ah! you remember the last verse," I said, entering, and speaking in a cheerful voice.

"Yes, yes," a little wearily. "I remember it, but I never sing it."

"Come, now, my child, try to bear it all patiently, and be cheerful."

"Oh! uncle, I try to, but every day my troubles seem to accumulate."

She then told me that Godfrey Laughton had been there that day, and had said that he *would marry her*, and that very shortly.

"I told him," said the brave girl, "that I would die first. He laughed derisively, saying: 'People didn't die so easily unless they were killed.' And he went on and said he had gone all lengths to get me, and that he would yet, and that he had already risked his very soul for this purpose. And uncle," speaking low and mysteriously, "I could lay my finger on the murderer of Gerald Gordon."

"Amy, my poor child, you are so excited that you know not what you are saying; come, let us go in."

She got up without speaking, and we entered the sitting-room together. I did not wish to return to the subject again, so I took my chair near the marble centre table, and commenced turning over some pictures which lay upon it. As I came near the last I found a little oil painting, which I picked up and examined closely. I found it to be one of Amy's taken in the costume of the Greek girl.

"I didn't know you had this, Amy; when was it taken?"

"Shortly after I made the dress for Lady Lillian's fancy party. Mamma knew the artist, and got him to paint two of these."

"Where is the other one?"

"Papa gave it to Gerald two days after the ball."

"I didn't know he had it at all," was my reply, as I dropped the subject and thought no more of it just then.

CHAPTER XXXII.

MRS. CARR, THE WATCH-TRINKET AND RAVINGS.

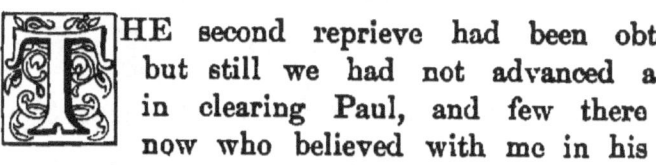HE second reprieve had been obtained, but still we had not advanced a step in clearing Paul, and few there were now who believed with me in his innocence. I was growing rapidly weary of life, and each day more and more despairing. When I saw the fall frosts carry away the last flowers, and the blasts of November came rushing in, chilling and killing all that was left of the beautiful summer, there was a dreary void in my heart which made me feel as if all were in vain. I rose one morning from the breakfast table, where I only went from habit, when one of the servants came in telling me that one of the tenants' wives was sick, and wished to see me.

I asked which one it was.

"Mrs. Carr, sir," he answered.

This Mrs. Carr lived half a mile from the dark grove on the upper end of the moorland.

I wrapped my cloak around me, and drew on my gloves, for it was bitter cold, and went forth. When I had crossed the park, and got out into the highway, I heard a voice calling me, and turning, saw Amy.

"Wait for me, uncle. I imagine we are both going in the same direction, and it will be so much nicer to have you than to be alone."

I kissed the cheeks that the cold blasts had tinged with a brilliant carmine.

"You are going to Mrs. Carr's, ain't you, uncle? I went to see her yesterday and found her very ill. I'm afraid she won't live."

"Has Lady Eleanor returned yet?" she asked, after we had walked some distance.

"No, no; not yet."

"You hear from them occasionally, don't you, uncle?"

"Yes, through Lord Gordon, though his health too is very delicate. His last letter with regard to poor Eleanor was not very cheering. He said her spirits were still very low and melancholy and nothing seemed to revive her."

We had now reached the tenant's door, which was opened by a chubby boy with red cheeks, red hair, and red hands. And to Amy's enquiry "How was his mother?" said, "He didn't know how his mother was; to ask her."

We went to the sick woman's bedside and found her in a very restless slumber. She presently opened her eyes and recognized us.

"Oh! is it you, Mr. Meredith and Miss Amy?" she asked, and her eyes closed again from sheer exhaustion.

We raised her head and poured a stimulant into her mouth, which she swallowed with difficulty. She then turned her face to me and said, in a weak voice:

"Mr. Meredith, it may be of some use to you: Godfrey Laughton passed my house at twelve o'clock at night on the 19th of August, 18—."

"In what direction?" I asked, breathlessly; but she turned her face to the wall and never spoke again.

I was stupified. Why had this woman sent for me to give me with her dying breath a piece of information which might turn the whole tide of affairs and bring my boy back into my arms once more? Perhaps this was the only evidence we could get, but now she was no more, and there was no one left to speak in the captive's cause.

"Was there no other grown person about the house on that night?" I enquired.

"No, there was no other there, the husband being absent."

Then all was as blank as ever, and when the neighbors came in to perform their duty to the dead, we arose and took our departure.

The sun was making a faint effort to shine as we passed out, but the glare was sickly and dim. We walked on for some time in silence, occupied with our own thoughts. The dark grove was but a short distance in front of us now, casting its black shadows around, and looking gloomier than ever. . One pale ray of the November sun was peeping through the opening the lightning had made on that dreadful night in August. It was an ill-shaped spot the ray formed, but it was bright and shining in contrast to the darkness of the rest of the scene. We both stood gazing on this particular place, where the body of the dead boy had laid. There was no mark left of that tragedy. The ground had long since drunk up the crimson blood which had watered the grass, and nothing now remained. Amy walked a few steps in front of me, and to my surprise entered the grove. She stooped down, and, on the place where the sunbeam played, picked up something.

"What is it, Amy?" I asked, hurriedly, but she walked rapidly on, as if to pass the dreary spot before answering me. She then turned and held towards me a small piece of jewelry, saying:

"Did Paul ever have anything like this?"

It was a small watch-trinket in the shape of a gaiter, with nine buttons composed of very fine brilliants. I examined it very closely, and did not recognize it. I felt sure that I had never seen it before. In answer to her enquiry, I said:

"Give it to me, child, and say nothing about it, for I must find out whom it belongs to."

We walked on then, both dreading to say anything, and fearing to hope. I knew by the tarnish on the little jewel that it must have been out some time. I took it with me to the Lodge and locked it carefully in my secretary, waiting until the next day before I proceeded further, for it was now late. My mind was so alive with this new hope that I slept very little during the night and rose bright and early the next morning. I pushed back my window curtain, and there before me was a white carpet, for it had snowed during the night as it can only snow in Merry England. The snow was still softly falling; the large fleecy flakes were coming down in myriads, gently and slowly. It had fallen on the tree tops, dressing the bare branches with a robe of virgin white, even the dark grove wearing a dress of spotless purity, and over the dreary moorland was a pure, smooth carpet, unbroken by a foot-print.

I stood there some time watching it, and thinking of the little trinket, when Patrick's head, rivaling the scene without in whiteness, peeped in, exclaiming:

"Why, are you up, masther? I thought to wake you, but here you are dressed."

"Yes, up and dressed. Any mail, Patrick?"

"Yes, a note and a letter."

"A note! From whom?"

"Dr. Arnold's servant gave it to me and told me to give it to you immediately."

I broke the note open hastily. It ran as follows:

DEAR FRIEND:

I am at the sick bed of Godfrey Laughton, and wish you to come here immediately, for strange things may be revealed.

Yours in haste,

T. J. ARNOLD.

I read the letter, which was from the old duke. It was full of kindness and sympathy, and trusting that we might still do something to liberate the prisoner. I was very much surprised when my eyes fell upon these words in the letter:

Yesterday, as I was passing by an artist's gallery, I entered to examine the pictures, and I was very much surprised to see a small oil painting of that very pretty girl, Miss Wayland, to whom you introduced me the last time I visited you. The picture is a very true and a very lovely one, and the costume it is taken in exceedingly becoming. The artist told me it was in the possession of Mr. Godfrey Laughton, who wished to have it remodeled.

How did this picture come into Godfrey Laughton's possession? I wondered, for I knew it was not the one at the cottage, for that I had seen but an evening or two before. It must have been the one Captain Wayland gave Gerald, and how did Godfrey Laughton get it? I thought of this and much more as I rode to his house. I was not long in arriving at my journey's end, and never was Merry Hall so quiet as it was this morning. The servants walked about noiselessly and spoke in whispers, and it altogether appeared very solemn. The butler took me into a warm sitting room, where a blazing fire burned in the grate, casting out a ruddy glow and making the apartment very comfortable. I asked for the doctor, and, taking a chair, sat looking into the red coals, wondering what the result of my visit here would be.

"A bitter cold morning, Meredith," said the doctor, coming in rubbing his hands. "How did you navigate through the snow? You didn't meet with an avalanche, did you?"

"Oh, no. I got on pretty well. How are you feeling to-day, doctor?"

"So-so," and drawing a chair up to the fire, he motioned me to come near to him.

I seated myself very close, and he leaned forward and commenced:

"Meredith, it has all been as I expected. I am an old man, and experience has given me much penetration, but I did not wish to hang a man on my suspicions merely and without some positive proof; but I have that now. The wild delirium made him tell a tale which was fearful, fearful. Could you have heard what I did through the still hours of the night the blood in your veins would have been frozen. It was he," pointing to the room above where the invalid was, "who severed the soul from the body under the firs."

I sprang to my feet and caught his arm.

"Doctor!"

"Be quiet, friend, be quiet. Much depends on our being calm."

He then motioned me to follow him, and led me up stairs into the patient's room. It was an elegantly furnished apartment, comfortable and luxurious, where not a breath of the winter wind dare enter; but I thought little of this as I approached the bed where lay the sick man, tossing restlessly, and unconscious. His handsome face was covered over with a scarlet mantle of fever and his eyes were wild and glaring. The doctor motioned me to a seat at the head of the bed and he took one on the opposite side. The invalid was muttering to himself, but I could not understand what he was saying, though I bent over and listened attentively. I waited a long time and had grown very tired. I raised myself up at last, thinking it was no use and that my kind friend must have been mistaken, but he nodded to me, and I resumed my former position. I had scarcely done so when I caught Gerald's name and "Those glaring eyes, why don't they"—then something followed that I could not understand, then some disconnected sentences were muttered like these:

"Blood stop flowing." "Little gaiter somewhere there." "Blood on picture and it won't wash out." "I'd kill a dozen to marry"—. "The gibbet will rid me of"—.

I waited long, but could catch no more. But I had heard enough.

"Will that confirm what I have told you," said the doctor, stooping over, and looking me in the eye.

I bowed my head and sat silent some time. The picture he spoke of must have been the one of Amy's that Gerald had, and the little gaiter the one she had found under the firs. As I thought of this I remembered that I had seen him hunting for something there some months before, and was struck at the time with the strangeness of the procceding.

I went with all haste back to the Lodge and dispatched to the duke to have the picture of Amy examined to see if there were any signs of blood upon it. I soon received a return telegram, saying the picture had been examined, but that there were no marks upon it. I was very much depressed at this and quite in a state of bewilderment, for if there were no trace of blood upon the picture, what right had we to pay attention to anything the sick man had said? The only thing that was left to cheer me now was the shoe, for he had spoken of that too in his delirium; but then I thought he might have dropped that at any other time. All my hopes seemed again blighted, and we could only wait now until the sick man recovered and see what steps we should take next. I was fully convinced, as was also Dr. Arnold, that Godfrey Laughton was the guilty one.

Old Patrick brought up my tea to my room that evening, for he used to sit with me now, and I was never weary of his companionship. I sat down to take a mouthful of the tea and a little toast, when the loud ring of the door-bell quite startled me, for this was something new in our quiet lives at the Lodge, where we never had visitors in the winter evenings.

"Who is it, Patrick?"

"I will go and see;" but scarcely had he reached the door when a servant entered and handed me a card. I was very much surprised to see the old duke's name upon it, and went down to the drawing-room where I found him warming his hands. There was another gentleman with him, to whom he introduced me as I entered. After a few common-place remarks, the duke said:

"Mr. Meredith, after the reception of your despatch, I was very much excited, and I went immediately and had the picture examined, which did not result in any discovery. When I returned to my room I could not rest, I was so anxious about it, and went the second time with more success. I had a very strong magnifying glass with which I had it examined closely, and we found a spot upon it, which, upon being analyzed, proved to be blood. I have brought the picture with me," he continued, walking to a table and taking it from a portfolio, and handing it to me.

I took it to the brilliant gaslight, but failed to detect the spot upon it.

"I see you do not perceive it," said the duke, "nor could I at first." He then pointed to one of the corners, where I saw for the first time a very tiny, faint spot, which many careful ablutions had almost obliterated. I looked at it long and earnestly, and wondered if this little spot, in its half circular dimensions, would be the means of proving Paul's innocence.

"Are you convinced of the nature of the stain?" spoke the duke, breaking my reverie. "It was some time before I myself was convinced, and if you have any doubts, this gentleman here will soon remove them on that score."

The gentleman alluded to bowed and was soon at work mixing his chemicals, which he shortly after applied to the spot, and I was no longer doubtful. I uttered a thanksgiving to God for His mercy.

"Now," said the duke, some time after, when the chemist had retired, "how did this painting come into Godfrey Laughton's hands, and how did the drop of blood come upon it? You have told me there were but two of this kind, one given to the young heir of Gordon and the other in Miss Wayland's own possession."

"Yes," I answered, "and this is certainly the one that was given to Gerald."

"Are you sure that Miss Wayland did not give the other to this Laughton herself?"

"As certain as I am that I am a living man, and to-morrow I shall prove it to you."

We retired then for the night. The next morning, very early, I had the close carriage ordered and went to the cottage for Amy. I told her my errand as soon as I arrived, and she made all possible haste to accompany me to the Lodge. We brought with us the other painting of Amy. I had just helped her into the carriage, and was getting into it myself, when young Lord Leigh rode up.

"Why, where are you bound for this unpleasant morning, my Lord?" I asked.

"After you, Mr. Meredith. I went to the Lodge and they told me you were here, so I came with all speed."

"Well, I'm glad I am found at last, my Lord, for it is a real pleasure to get a glimpse of you these days. Just give your horse to the out-rider and jump in here with us; we will both be delighted to have you, eh, Amy?"

"Yes, indeed, uncle, that we will; so insist upon Lord Leigh's coming in here and making himself comfortable."

It was not necessary to urge him further; he jumped from his horse upon hearing her voice, and went to the carriage door, saying:

"So, Miss Amy, you are out in the cold, too; this is what mother would call, 'braving the lion in his den.' I feel myself very much like the 'old woman wrapped up in the blanket,'" trying to extricate his hands from the wrappings around him, "but this is not my fault, Miss Amy, I did it to oblige mamma, who would think my ears would be frost-bitten if I did not obey her."

"And your mamma is right—but just hear the bells, the silver bells," she broke off, looking out the window as several sleighs passed by.

"I don't want to hear them again, for yesterday I was riding with poor little Lillian and the sleigh upset, and I made a vow that I would never sleigh-ride any more."

"That you will break some of these days, and I suspect before the snow will leave," answered Amy.

We had now arrived at the Lodge, and Lord Leigh jumped from the carriage and assisted Amy out. After

I had introduced Amy into the sitting-room where the duke was, I drew Lord Leigh apart and told him what had passed. Whilst I spoke his eyes sparkled, and he seemed all eagerness to begin with the evidence we had to clear the prisoner. I then told the duke that we had better commence at once to take down the notes, as Lord Leigh's time was limited.

I went up stairs for the picture which the duke had brought, and which I had put into my secretary the night before. As I took it from its resting-place, I drew with it the little gold shoe. I hastily picked it up and went down stairs with it in my hand. When I went into the room the company gathered around me. I handed the picture to the duke, who gave it to Amy, saying:

"Do you recognize this?"

"Of course I do, my Lord," said the girl, innocently. "This is one of two pictures that was painted for me in July, 18—."

"Well, how did you dispose of this one?" he asked.

"I did not dispose of it myself. My father gave it to Gerald, heir of Gordon, shortly after it was taken."

"But, my child," said the old man, "could you swear that this was the one?"

"Yes," she returned, "there were only two of them," and she walked to the piano, where her muff and gloves lay, and brought the corresponding picture.

The duke took the two pictures in his hands.

Besides," said Amy, "there was another mark or two by which I would know the one that papa gave away from mine. There was a scratch across the neck, made by mamma's shawl-pin, which mamma thought disfigured it greatly, and she was glad it was that one that papa gave to Gerald."

We all looked eagerly at the picture and saw there the scratch which she had described.

"And besides this mark, there were three Arabic characters on the back of the canvass, which Paul painted in Indian ink one evening. I don't know what they stand for, though," she continued.

We turned the picture and looked at the back, and there saw very plainly the three characters which she had told us of, and we all felt now perfectly satisfied as to the identity of the picture.

The duke then asked if there was anyone present when her father gave this away, and she answered:

"Yes, Mr. Laughton."

He then looked at me significantly and I returned his glance. I raised up from the table on which I had been leaning, and, in doing so, knocked the little trinket to the floor. Lord Leigh stooped and picked it up. He looked at it long and curiously.

"My Lord," I asked, whilst my heart palpitated very rapidly, "did you ever see that before?"

"Yes, Mr. Meredith."

"Where, my Lord?"

"On Godfrey Laughton's watch-chain. It was given to him by a friend of mine and I was present when it was presented."

"Have you seen him wear it very lately?" I asked, coming close to him.

"No, I hav'nt seen it for some time, and I was very much surprised when I picked it up here on the floor."

"How long has it been since you saw it? Think, my Lord," said the duke, earnestly.

"I do not exactly know, but think it has been some time. I was always attracted by it, it is such a pretty little thing."

"And you do not remember how long it has been since you saw Godfrey Laughton wear it?" asked Amy, anxiously.

He studied a while, turning the gaiter over in his hands, and then said:

"Yes, I do remember now, perfectly. We were hunting together on the eighteenth of August, the day before the dreadful tragedy. His horse jumped a fence, and his watch, which was carelessly placed in his vest pocket, fell out and hung by the chain, and this little trinket became detached and dropped to the ground. He got off his horse to look for it, and I, too, assisted in the hunt. I found it, after some time, by the brilliancy of the stones shining amongst some leaves. As I handed it to him he said it had a trick of falling from his chain, and he must go the next week to a jeweler and have it made secure."

"And this is positively the last time you saw it?"

"Positively, the last," was the answer. "It looks, though," he added, "as if it had been very badly treated. Mr. Meredith, where did you get it?"

I answered—

"That Amy had found it in the grove of firs on the moorland. And what do you think of it?" I concluded.

"That we have found the assassin."

CHAPTER XXXIII.

THE CONVICTION OF GODFREY LAUGHTON.

OLD Dr. Arnold called to see me one morning at the Lodge, and when I went to meet him said:

"He is plenty able now to stand his trial, and moody enough he looks about it, too."

"Are you sure, doctor, that our chain of evidence is complete?"

"Complete enough, my friend, to clear the innocent and condemn the guilty."

"Then, this is Tuesday, and fourteen days from to-day comes the trial?"

"Yes, yes," answered the doctor, "and you will have Paul back with you again, which will be just cause for you to be happy."

Since the events of our last chapter, we had gotten several other convincing proofs of Godfrey's guilt. I had not heard from Lord Gordon for two or three months, and, as I had said when speaking to Amy, his last letter was sad and gloomy as regarded Eleanor. On this morning, when the doctor left me, I took the pony chaise and rode to the office myself. A letter was handed me, which I saw was from Lord Gordon. I broke the seal and read:

DEAR JOHN:

am in great trouble about poor Eleanor. She has never recovered from the effects of that dreadful night which robbed us of our son. Her mind has been fearfully impaired. You know I insisted upon a change of climate and a change of scene; but all has been in vain. On Tuesday evening last I noticed a great change in her for the worse; her eyes were wild and staring, and she scarcely spoke to me; would eat nothing, and drove her maid from her presence altogether. A friend called to see me, and I was obliged to leave her for a little while. When I returned she was absent, and when I enquired of the servants if they knew where their mistress was, their answers were all in the negative. I could not gain the slightest information from any one. I have searched everywhere and am still searching, but it seems fruitless. I trust you above all others, and I wish you would make enquiries. I have heard of the suspicions which rest upon Laughton. I am very much relieved, for I never could think that it was Paul that had robbed me of my only child. I told Eleanor about it, but she did not speak, and I could not tell how it affected her. Remember me kindly to Paul, and believe me your sincere friend,

GERALD LORD GORDON.

I was very much troubled when I read this letter. All Eleanor's bright prospects had come to this. I was still musing upon it when a boy came up and handed me a telegram, saying:

"This has just come for you, sir."

It ran as follows:

MR. JOHN MEREDITH:

A lady supposed to be Lady Eleanor Gordon was taken up a raving maniac this morning and lodged in the Asylum at M——.

(Signed) WALTER KEAN, M. D.,
of Asylum M——.

I went instantly to the ticket-office and bought a ticket for M——, wrote a short note to Dr. Arnold explaining my absence, and was soon *en route*. Before starting I sent a telegram to Lord Gordon acquainting him with Eleanor's whereabouts. I gazed upon the wintry sky as the railway carriage hurried on and thought that my life was quite as overcast as it was, my comforts few, my trials many, but if Paul could be saved now, the rest of my days promised peace.

I soon reached my destination. Having no baggage, I jumped to the platform, and calling a hackman, who was throwing his hands around his body to keep them from freezing, engaged him to drive me to the asylum.

I found Doctor Kean a very nice gentleman, and he expressed himself greatly relieved that I had come. He said that he thought Lady Gordon very ill and a very bad case; she was raving a great deal.

"I did not know where her husband was or I would have sent for him also," he said.

"How did she get here?" I asked. "It is at least a hundred and twenty miles distant from where her husband is."

"She came by the early morning train, but was not so bad when she first arrived, and stopped at the hotel, where she ordered rooms. Some of her friends recognized her there and asked her where her husband was. She said she had killed him, and this was the first intimation they had of her condition. I was sent for immediately, and found her perfectly insane. I dispatched at once for you, knowing you to be her relative."

"I am very much indebted to you, sir; but cannot I see the patient now?"

"Certainly," and he led the way to the ward in which Eleanor was located.

She was lying on a bed, raving painfully. When I spoke to her she did not at all recognize me. She called incessantly upon the name of her dead child. I was deeply grieved for her. There was no longer a trace of the beautiful woman of old. She had torn out her soft, fair hair by the handfuls and scratched her smooth, transparent skin until it was terribly disfigured. Lord Gordon came early the next morning, but she was as unconscious of his presence as she was of mine. He wished to take her to the Lodge, but the doctor persuaded him to let her remain.

On the following Monday week I was again seated in the court-room, but under very different circumstances from the time that I was there before. I was a witness against the prisoner at the bar, who was Godfrey Laughton. The most of the evidence against him you have heard; but the most convincing was that of two women from the Hall, one of them the nurse during the prisoner's illness and the other the assistant. They had been compelled to go into his private wardrobe for some linen whilst he was sick and found there a shirt and a pair of linen pants, hidden away under some other things, which were stained with blood of long standing. It was remembered by his servants that he had worn a pair of pants that answered to the description of these on the evening of the 19th of August, 18—. The servants also gave evidence that he was not at the Hall on that unhappy evening from about six until one at night. The evidence against him was very great and convincing, and the verdict pronounced him "*guilty.*"

* * * * * * *

What a happy party we were at Lady Grantley's when Paul was free and with us once more. Amy looked lovelier than ever, and the airy, fairy Lillian was as blight as a bird. Anthony's surname was more appropriate than before, and Lord Leigh's handsome face was wreathed with smiles and thankfulness, whilst Paul, who was pale and thin, poor boy, but as handsome as ever, was very happy. Lady Grantley, the kind old duke, the doctor, and myself sat a little apart watching them, with our hearts overflowing in thanksgiving.

But I must forget ourselves here for a little while, and give you the prisoner's history and confession, which he had written and left us.

CHAPTER XXXIV.

HISTORY AND CONFESSION OF THE MURDERER.

 WAS born in Bingen on the 14th May, 18—, and was the third son of a large family. My father was an honest, industrious mechanic, and my mother pious and amiable. At an early age I showed talent and vivacity and was considered remarkably handsome. My mother indulged me very much. She was proud of my fair face and graceful carriage, and made her other children succumb to my every wish. We were very poor, and my two older brothers had to toil for their daily bread. But I was a little idler, who refused to do anything and was never compelled.

"I remember, when I was about eleven years old, my father was employed building some frame stores for a rich merchant, and would go to his work very early every morning and not return until late in the evening. My mother called me to her one day and asked me if I would take my father's dinner to him; that all the other children were absent. I said, 'I reckoned so,' and being tired of nothing to do, picked up the basket that contained his meal and went to where he was working. I was always bland to strangers, and as a general thing attracted them. When I arrived at the place where my father was, I found him speaking to a handsomely-dressed gentleman. So, wearing a most winning smile, I bowed low and handed my father his dinner. The stranger eyed me complacently, and asked:

" ' Is this your son ? '

" ' Yes,' answered my father, feeling flattered that I was thus noticed.

" ' You are a fine little boy. Have you ever been to school?' said the gentleman, patting me on the head.

" ' No, sir.'

" ' Would you like to go?' he asked.

" ' Ah! indeed that I would, sir, above all things,' I answered.

" ' Why, this is ambition, and that's what I glory in.'

" Then turning to my father he said:

" ' If you will let me have this boy of yours I will educate him as a gentleman, and when he grows older will give him a fine berth in my mercantile establishment.'

" My father was so overpowered with gratitude and delight that he could scarcely speak, and stroked my face most lovingly. The stranger then asked me:

" ' How would you like that, my boy?'

" ' Nothing would give me such pleasure; I would be more than delighted—and you are so very kind,' kissing his hand.

" He seemed greatly pleased with me, and told me to go home now and tell my mother, and that he would come for me on the morrow.

" I bade him adieu, and ran all the way home, full of the idea of being a gentleman. When I told my mother she wept very bitterly, and said she could not bear to give me up, calling me all the while the most endearing names. I told her that she did not know what was good for me, that it was all glorious, and went to bed that night with visions of the future as bright as sunbeams. I waked early next morning, and found that my mother had staid up all night to wash and arrange my scanty wardrobe. As the day advanced she kissed me again and again, and begged God to bless me. When the time of parting came, my brothers bade me good-bye with tears in their honest eyes, whilst mine remained unmoistened. My little sister was perhaps the only one I parted from with any regret. She was so beautiful, and had been such a willing little slave to me, and I felt that I would miss her very much. I bade her adieu with a tear which was soon dried, and as the sun sank on 'fair Bingen,' I left my paternal roof.

"The old gentleman took me kindly by the hand when I was telling my father good-bye, thinking that I would feel the parting, but the sorrow was all on one side. 'Good-bye, Oscar, my son, good-bye; don't forget your old father, my child, who loves you so fondly.' He kissed my cheeks whilst the big tears fell fast upon them, but I was unmoved. The stranger then put me in his carriage, and shaking hands with my parents jumped in after me. The last words I ever heard my father say were: 'Oscar, my son, don't forget me.'

"I was not at all abashed before the strange man, for I was never afraid of strangers, and talked a great deal, which seemed to please the gentleman, for he encouraged me in it.

"He had a fine outfit made for me during the next

week or two and sent me to one of the German colleges, where I remained seven years. I was smart, ambitious and brilliant, and stood first in all my classes, and at eighteen was considered sufficiently capable of taking my stand in the mercantile house. My old patron was very kind to me, and seemed very proud that I had succeeded so well. After my return to Bingen, I was installed as head clerk in one of his establishments. My kind friend was never weary of serving my interests. I made myself as agreeable to him as possible and feigned an unusual amount of gratitude.

"One evening as I was pouring over some accounts, my benefactor came in, and said:

"'Oscar, my boy, I hear you have not been to see your family yet; put up those books and go to them, boy.'

"I was ashamed to confess that it was pride that had prevented me from visiting them, and made the excuse that it was 'press of business.'

"'Make that an excuse no longer, Oscar, for I want you to pay a visit to them every day.'

"I was half angry at this, for I would rather not have visited the scenes where I had once been a poor carpenter's son. But I thanked the old man with well-assumed gratitude, and, shutting up my books, walked out. I soon found myself in the narrow street where my mother dwelt—my father having long since died. I hesitated some time before I would enter this humble dwelling where I was born, and where those that should have been dearest to me were living. I was on the point of turning back, when a desire to see my beautiful sister caused me to change my mind, so I rapped at the door and it was opened to me by the lovely girl I had just wished to see. I did not at first recognize her, nor she me. I told her who I was, and said, 'I wished to see my mother.'

"She threw her arms around my neck, and called me her dear, dear brother, asking if I had come back to them again after so long an absence. I kissed her rosy lips, and felt very proud of her, because she had been true to her girlhood, and had grown into a lovely woman. She then took me in to my mother, and said, 'here, mother, is Oscar come back to us once more.' My kind mother cried with delight when she found out who I was, and pressed me to her heart repeatedly, shedding tears of joy. When my brothers came home from work they both met me very affectionately, but I inwardly shrank from them, for they were in their working clothes, and I had a sinful pride as regarded such things. When I arose to go, my mother pleaded with me to remain with them during the night. I looked at the poor beds around and smiled, simply thanked her, and said that business would not allow.

"'Then come back to see me often, dearest,' she urged, as I was leaving.

"'Ah! do,' joined in my sister, whom I kissed lovingly, for she was so very, very pretty.

"But a few months passed away when I became very tired of clerking, and wondered why I could not be like my master, with plenty of money and nothing to do. These thoughts haunted my brain day and night, and I was continually asking myself the question, 'How could I accomplish it?' Yet every cent I received I spent in gambling saloons, in pleasure, and for dress. I never thought of bestowing a farthing upon my mother and sister, who, as I before said, were very poor. I was too fond of my own ease and comfort. On one of my visits home, I found my sister absent. When I asked where she was, my mother smiled, and said, 'that she was walking with a friend.'

"'Who is this friend?' I enquired.

"'A very nice and respectable young mechanic, and well worthy of the affections of my child,' she replied.

"'What do you mean, mother; that there is a betrothal existing between them?'

"'Yes, my son, that is it.'

"I bit my lips with vexation. I had a boon companion to whom I intended marrying my sister. I felt sure that he could not resist her exceeding loveliness, and besides, she had a thousand little winning ways that would captivate the most fastidious. I determined in some way to get rid of this 'nice and respectable young mechanic.' During the course of the visit, my sister returned with her accepted suitor. He was very handsome, with a frank, honest face, and eyes which spoke volumes of love for the exquisite girl—my sister. I never saw her look more charming than she did then, her delicately chiseled face wreathed in the happiest smiles, and her eyes beaming brightly. I bowed very coldly to the young man, and embraced my sister as they came in. I did not remain long after this, but left the house vowing that an estrangement should soon take place between this young couple. I very soon after this introduced my bosom friend to my family; he was on a par with myself, and was very soon enamored of my sister's charms. I determined that she should marry him, but she gave him no encouragement, which enraged us both. We made up our minds to dispatch my friend's rival as soon as possible. It was on a summer evening that we had planned to meet him, as he was returning from his work on the outskirts of the city, and it was arranged that I should insult him, and a duel would ensue, in which I promised myself every advantage. A demon urged me, and on I went. We met, and in every possible way I provoked him. At first, he bore with me very calmly, but at length his temper was roused, and he took the pistol I proffered, and said he would fight. I would not allow him time to call a second, but made my companion measure the ground, and we took our stand, the signal was given and we fired, and my sister's affianced husband fell dead upon the grass. The blue Rhine flowed murmuringly along as if to chide me for my evil deed, and I fled from the spot, my companion following me, without being either pursued or suspected. I never forgot the next evening when I called at my mother's home. There lay my sister cold and motionless, with a broken heart; she never smiled again, nor spoke to any of us; she turned from me instinctively as if she knew I was the cause of all her sorrow, and three weeks from that day I followed her to her home in the churchyard. For a

time I felt a great grief, but it wore away at last. The
suspicions of the murder never rested upon me, but I
thought it would be better for me to be far away from
my native land. The spirits of the two beings I had
sent to an early grave were continually haunting me,
and I determined to leave—but how was I to accomplish this without friends or money? At length, I
concluded to forge a check upon my benefactor's house.
I soon after put this determination into execution, and
found myself in possession of fifty thousand pounds,
and on the evening of that same day, after passing the
churchyard to cast one more glance on the grave of my
poor sister, I left the vine clad hills as the setting sun
was bathing them in a rosy twilight forever. I
assumed a disguise that was so complete, that I was
never recognized. After a time, I went over into Ireland, where I became acquainted with Captain Wayland, and assisted him in his elopement with Miss
Oswald, and he and I have been boon companions ever
since. I soon became tired of Ireland, and came over
into England, and adopted the manners and costume
of the Englishman, as well as his country, leading as
gay a life as possible to banish the phantoms of the
past. This I had nearly done; time passed away and
all seemed to be going on well, when Amy Wayland
arrived from Paris. I had never loved in all my
life, but she was so winning, so lovely, and so gentle,
that I soon became captive to her womanly graces and
charms; her image was constantly before me, and I
loved her wildly and passionately. When I heard she
was betrothed to Paul Stewart, I became almost fran-

tic, and the night of Lady Grantly's ball, I heard the conversation between him and Amy, and bit my lips until the blood flowed. (I loved her so, that I would not bring her name before the public court, although I knew it was she to whom Paul was speaking—I preferred perjuring myself.) I also heard the conversation between Lady Gordon and Captain Wayland the same night, and I knew this was the stronger party, and was the one to fear. I was confident, though, that Amy loved Paul, so I resolved then and there to get rid of my two rivals. I never liked Gerald Gordon— poor, weak boy—but now I hated him, as I thought he would be successful. I liked Stewart infinitely better, but I consigned him to a far worse fate, thinking that Amy would cease to love him when she heard him branded as a felon. You all know when the engagement between Gerald and Amy was made public. I vowed then to murder him and bring evidence so strong against Paul Stewart that he would be indicted. The night of the 19th of August came at last, the next sun would shine upon the marriage day, and this was my last chance for action; now, how was I to commit the deed without being suspected myself? I had been thinking about it for a whole week. You all remember that in my evidence I told you that I found Paul Stewart standing beneath one of the trees not far from the grove on that night. I knew he was mourning over his sad fate, and that in his heart there raged a tempest as fearful as the one in which he stood. He did not mind the pelting rain, the muttering thunder, or the vivid lightning, they accorded but too well with his own feelings; but my heart palpitated wildly when I saw him. I knew that Gerald Gordon had not returned from B———, for I had made all enquiries. So, after bidding Drew good night, under the pretence of hastening home, I passed across the lower end of the moorland, tied my horse in a thicket beyond, and hurried back, but here I met with an obstruction; I was obliged to pass by Mrs. Carr's cabin, the door was open and a stream of light fell in my path; the woman was at the door, and her keen eye recognizing me, she asked me where I was going in such a storm.

"I walked rapidly on without answering, hoping that she would imagine herself mistaken. I first went to the spot where I had left Paul Stewart, and, to my satisfaction, found him gone. I then entered the grove of firs, and did not have to wait very long until I heard Gerald Gordon's horse coming towards me. I called up all my courage here. His horse, generally so restive and fiery, was as tractable as a lamb. I caught it by the bridle as it came up to me, and threw it back on its haunches. A demon's strength was in my arms. I then jerked the rider from its back. He struggled manfully, but I struck him a blow on his head with my pistol, which stunned him. I pulled him some distance into the grove. He then returned to consciousness and asked, 'Who wishes to kill me?' and by a lightning flash saw my face, and said, 'Is it you, Godfrey?' I cocked my pistol. He here begged, for pity sake, to let him pray one moment for mercy. He raised himself upon his knees and said, 'For God's sake, don't kill me.' I pointed my pistol, and as he cried 'Lord have mercy' I fired, and he fell upon the grass. I then searched in one pocket for the picture of Amy Wayland, which I had seen him have that very morning, and which he showed me on his way to town, and irritated me by asking 'if I would not like to have it.' It was the only thing he possessed that I coveted, for when I could not have Amy with me, I must have this representation of her. So I quickly concealed it in my pocket, and ran in the direction of my horse, which I soon mounted, and hastened to the Hall. I put the horse away myself, for fear of detection. I then opened the Hall door with a night-key, and went softly up to my chamber. There was my room all prepared by the careful servants; the lamp was lighted; the curtains all drawn to. I doubly locked the door when I entered. I looked at my clothes; they were stained with blood. I drew them off hurriedly, wrapped them up, and put them in a wardrobe which no one entered but myself. The painting I also hid. I then washed my hands again and again, and took a bath in my bath-room, and threw out the water myself, so that none would be the wiser. I could not sleep that night, for I could see the dead boy's face peering at me from every corner of the room. I was afraid to look in any direction. I shut my eyes, but it was all the same. I dared not walk up and down my chamber floor, for the very sound of my footsteps were like echoes from the tomb, and in every shadow cast upon the ceiling or wall I could see the murdered boy's dying eyes, and every sigh of the night-wind seemed to bear upon its breath his last words. As the dawn began to break, I sought my bed to avoid suspicion, and I parried it for a long time. I was very much alarmed when I found my little watch-trinket was gone, for I knew it must have fallen that night near the grove, and this kept me in a wretched state of suspense for many days. But as time passed away I thought less of it, though I hunted for it frequently. The stain of blood on the picture annoyed me unceasingly. I washed it and washed it until I thought it had disappeared altogether. I was so crazy to have it remodeled that I sent it to London, and you all know the consequences. And the few remaining items of my life you are also acquainted with. I have been a wicked man, but my retribution will be very great. Amy Wayland's image has lived with me and will go with me down to the grave. I dare not ask for pity, for I know you have none to give; but did I know that only one tear would fall for me, I would die happier."

This ended the history and the confession, and when we read it, we did not refuse him the tears he sighed for.

CONCLUSION.

THE following June, at the little country church, as the evening sunbeams stole in through the windows, casting their bright rays on the altar and the pictures, two bridal couples entered—and handsomer couples could not be found in all England. I am sure it will not be hard for my reader to guess who they were. The first that knelt and received the blessing of the old priest was Lord Leigh and his "airy, fairy Lillian," who looked lovelier than ever in her bridal robes. The next were my two adopted children, and as I heard the words, "what God has joined together let no man put asunder," I leaned my head upon the railing and wept with joy.

Nine halcyon years have passed since then, and we are now back in old Erin, at my childhood's home. All seems the same here on this summer eve as in days gone by. The flowers are budding and blooming, exhaling their rich perfumes; the fountains are still playing, whispering sweet music as the crystal drops fall into the basin; the silvery Shannon is still murmuring and complaining on to the sea; and Nature is as lavish with her gifts as she was when I was a child and *she* was a child.

Paul and Amy are noble, loving, and good, and are truly happy. No furrows mark the brow of my young hero—it is as placid as the summer sea—and his little wife is a perfect sunbeam. I walk with a stick now, and the great mirror opposite tells me that my locks are as white as the snow; but I am just as happy as happy can be, and fear that I am a spoiled old man, as Amy does everything for me. She even parts and smooths my silvery hair, and tells me, laughing, that it looks much prettier after it is touched by her magic fingers.

Captain Wayland died three years after Amy's marriage, and, I think, was quite repentant. Old Patrick's green grave lies where the silvery waters of the river he loved so well sing to him night and morning. I can see the mound from here, and the myrtle and the roses are twining gracefully over it. There, too, is a monument that rises over a grave bearing the name of Nita. This grave has been carefully attended, and is a beautiful little spot in itself.

The old duke is still living, but he is very aged. I manage to pay him a visit annually, as he requests it, and I am generally accompanied by Amy and Paul.

Lord Leigh and Lillian spend many a pleasant day with us, and so does Anthony, as gay as ever, whose coming we all hail with joy. He is still fancy free, and laughingly says that Paul and Leigh married the only women he ever wanted.

Poor Eleanor died in the asylum soon after being received there. Lord Gordon lives a lonely life at the Lodge. He seems to care for no one but me. He often sends for me to come to him, and says that my visits are the only ones that cheer him.

The moon is now peeping up from behind the hills, leaving its golden track upon the waters. The night-birds are singing in the distant woods, and as it is getting late, I must bid adieu to my manuscript. But just down here in the yard is a little figure clothed in spotless muslin, while the night breezes are lifting the brown curls from her fair forehead. I look down and ask her, "Nita, my little pet, what are you doing?" She throws me a kiss from her cherry lips with her tiny hand, saying, "Helping little Johnnie water my grandmama's Nile lilies, you darling old uncle."

THE END.

www.ingramcontent.com/pod-product-compliance
Lightning Source LLC
Chambersburg PA
CBHW032054220426
43664CB00008B/989